THE GR

George Carey w
of London. H
churchgoing family but discovered
the Christian faith in his late teens. After
National Service in the RAF he went to the
London College of Divinity to train for the
Anglican ministry and subsequently took Bache-
lor, Master and Doctoral degrees at London
University. He has served on the staff of three
theological colleges and for a period of five years
was Principal of Trinity Theological College,
Bristol. In 1987 he was appointed Bishop of
Bath and Wells. A respected author, he has
written seven books on various subjects – Christ-
ology, the Church, Ministry, Humanity and
God. He is convinced that often the Church gets
in the way of God and strives for a warmhearted,
compassionate and selfless Christianity which
will let God be God.

He is happily married to Eileen who is a great
support and friend and they have four grown-up
children who keep them earthed in laughter and
normal life.

THE
GREAT GOD
ROBBERY

George Carey

Collins
FOUNT PAPERBACKS

First published in Great Britain by
Fount Paperbacks, London in 1989

Copyright © George Carey 1989

Printed and bound in Great Britain by
William Collins Sons & Co. Ltd, Glasgow

Contents

Introduction

That God is news is something we all know. He seems to pop up all the time – in our newspapers, in politics and in daily life. Yet curiously enough for many in western culture, he is the great irrelevance in our lives. Why is this? On the one hand, the case for the existence of God is strong; there are many intelligent people who do not find the idea of a personal God at all at odds with their knowledge of the world and universe. Indeed, they find him the integrating factor in human experience and knowledge. We might conclude from this that all that remains is for those who believe to convince those who do not. The problem is, I argue, that our western culture has done us a serious disservice – it has so robbed us of the sense of the transcendent that we are unable to give due attention to the question of God. Our world is a one-dimensional grey world bereft of mystery, awe and wonder. It is not surprising therefore that we find ourselves scoffing at those with strong beliefs yet wistfully envying their certainties and convictions. I hope then that this small book, written in the context of an extremely busy life, and probably showing all the marks of it, will be a help to those who thoughtfully return to the big question again: Is there a God? And if there is, how can we make contact with him?

For the sake of the general reader I have deliberately departed from the convention of footnotes. At the end of the book I have appended some of my sources and make suggestions for further reading. I trust that this decision will be of assistance to the person who simply wants to read the text and does not want to be told the number of books the author has press-ganged into his service!

I want to express my appreciation to all those who made this book possible. I am grateful to Sarah Baird-Smith of Collins Publishers Ltd for her patience and encouragement; for the Hockerill Educational Trust who made it possible for me to study at Tantur Ecumenical Institute in Jerusalem where most of the preparatory work was done; and for my son, Andrew, who read over the manuscript and made some constructive remarks and saved me from some amusing howlers. I take the blame for any he did not spot!

1

The Great "God" Robbery

The 64,000 dollar question is not, "Can you lend me 64,000 dollars?", but "Is there a God?" That is, can modern intelligent men and women *seriously* accept rationally that there is a divine Creator of this mysterious and fascinating universe who loves us and wants to enter into a relationship with us? There is no denying the urgency of such a question because the future as well as the credibility of Christianity rests upon the answer we give. How can we preach that Jesus Christ is the answer to our needs if there is a major question concerning the existence of the Father to whom he pointed? I know of many people who are attracted to the person of Christ but who raise fundamental questions about God himself. They look at the world and their experience of it and say: "I see much which makes me disbelieve in such a divine being – the inexplicable tragedies which happen to others, the random nature of things which does not suggest a Planner, the cruelty and rapaciousness of nature. Can a kind, benevolent Creator be behind such a place as this?"

This book is written to tackle such questions directly and honestly. I do so because I too have had to wrestle with them and still do. If it is any comfort to others, I have never found it easy to believe in God. Even though I am a bishop in the Church of England, honesty requires me to say that my search for him and my finding of him have not been simple or painless. There have been times of great agonising doubt but I have never lost sight of the need to come to a decision on this important issue. *If* there is a God who can be known and experienced, then the consequences for us are exciting indeed. They will affect our personal life and behaviour as well as our corporate experience. If there is no personal God behind the things that are, we must equally face up to the implications of living in a universe in which there is only ultimate futility and purposelessness. This does not negate what happinesses or meaning we may care to thrust into life, but it would signify that all of life is on a slide which takes us down to blackness and nothingness. The consequences of this belief affect all we are and what we do.

My own investigations over a period of many years have given me a quiet assurance that there is a God who has given us sufficient clues in life, nature, human thought, beauty and art to satisfy the genuine enquirer that he exists, and that he has expressed himself most meaningfully in Jesus Christ. However, you may come to a different conclusion at the end of this study and that is your right as a thinking responsible person. All I can do is to invite you to join me in looking at the arguments again, to consider whether you agree that there are sufficient reasons for us to believe in a "divine" being who is "out there" as well as "with us" – a "Being" who has created the universe and still pours his creativity into it. I would like to think that, as well as the thinking enquirer who may read this book, it will be of help to Christians who just want to be reminded of the great truths of the Christian faith. I hope it will encourage you and make you more confident as a Christian today.

But before we get to work there is one fact we must face up to — the scepticism of western society when it comes to believing in God. Such scepticism is not the result of honest reflection and argument which has led to agnosticism but rather the opposite — unthinking conclusions which emanate from assumptions current in our society. This came home to me with great force when I was once interviewing a young prisoner in a Remand Centre. When I mentioned God, he scoffed and said "Well, nobody believes in God these days do they!" I asked him to give me one good reason why I should not and he fell silent in helpless confusion unable to give one coherent thought to back up his remark. What he was doing, actually, was expressing an attitude not an argument. He is not alone. Western society through its ceaseless search for materialistic prosperity has created a climate which makes it difficult for us to comprehend the supernatural. Agnosticism has been present in all cultures since mankind started to think about ultimate questions but what is totally novel is the fact of agnostic culture itself which creates a climate of unbelief insidious in its effects and consequences. So, for the genuine enquirer or believer, it feels like running up an escalator which is coming down because the assumptions of our society are naturalistic and this worldly and dismissive of ideas which do not "ring cash registers", "build houses" or result in something "practical". God has been marginalised, not by thought or argument, but by the consequences of pragmatic attitudes to life which have had their effect in every area of human living.

In short we have become conceptual "Philistines". We have moved away from the really big questions such as Kant's great trio of questions which concluded his *Critique of Pure Reason*: What can I know? What ought I to do? What may I hope for? Instead, the whole sweep of creative conceptual thinking outlined in Kant's questions, which I believe stands behind human nature as moral, spiritual and eternal, has been shattered into a million fragments, reducing the life and destiny of mankind to an unattractive, grey materialism.

This is not, indeed, to deny the rich contribution that science, and technology in particular, has made to human progress. None of us wishes to return to a past, void of the fruits of scientific achievement. We all recognise that the last hundred years have seen a revolution in the history of mankind and we are generally thankful for it. What I am pointing out is the loss of the great ideological questions. Unless you are a religious person or perhaps someone with a strong ideology you will not have anything greater than yourself to believe in. No longer dwarfed by questions about the transcendent, no longer awed and thrilled by the wonder of creation, we have settled for an attitude to life which is basically functional and materialistic. The message fed to us from birth is that there are no transcendent questions to bother about. Rather, the really important issues concern this life: our standard of living, our professional careers, the education of our children and so on. So, we live in an age in which the divine, at least in its classical forms, has receded into the background of human concerns and consciousness. We have been "robbed of God" not by coming to such a conclusion after careful, considered, reflective thought but by acquired attitudes, assumptions and transferred values of a culture which is conditioning us not to believe.

Three important aspects of this "robbing" need to

be noted. First, there is the SEPARATION of the
individual from his or her community. We are told
repeatedly that one of the glories of Western civilisation
is the place given to the individual person resulting in
greater freedom of choice and opportunities for personal
fulfilment. While I have no wish to deny the obvious
benefits of our civilisation we have to point out the
negative elements within the process of individuation.
Take the claim that we have greater freedom to choose.
Is this the case? It seems otherwise when we begin to
analyse the situation. The process of modern life has led
to the weakening of the all-embracing and all-sustaining
communities of pre-Industrial society. Modern people
are now more mobile, more anonymous, free to belong to
and to choose what kind of society they wish to identify
with. But the paradox is that at the same time, the
sophistication of modern life has led to the replacement
of the communities which used to have such influence
over individuals by abstract megastructures which are
more anonymous and controlling than anything that
preceded them. The "global village" of the modern
world means that, unbeknown to most of us, our lives,
our leisure, our patterns of eating and drinking and the
values we cherish, are influenced most profoundly by
forces beyond ourselves. The irony therefore is that it
has led to less freedom of choice. A clear example of
this in present day Britain is our media which used to be
proudly extolled as an example of a free and independent
source of communication. Few would claim that nowa-
days. As a diocesan bishop, and therefore a little closer
to the centre of news distribution than I used to be,
I have become alarmed by the way the public is controlled, protected, and even sometimes manipulated by

those who have such power over the media. It is inevitable, then, that our beliefs about life and death and our value judgements are going to be shaped by what we read and see.

Then there is the process of SECULARISATION which is the consequence of many complex factors which include the impact of industrialisation, the Enlightenment and the failure of the churches to communicate the essence of Christianity. Without the individual being consciously aware of it, this movement constitutes a massive threat to an appreciation of the transcendent in human existence. Now, what do we mean by "secularisation"? I mean by this term a process of change within society, either deliberate or unconscious, which leaves God out, electing for the material in preference to the spiritual, the worldly over and against eternal values. The process of secularisation appears complete when supernatural faith becomes private and optional. In many developed countries this process appears almost complete but the result is serious for the individual and community. It is not only religious thinkers who recognise that secularisation frustrates deeply grounded aspirations in the heart of the average man and woman whose natural desire is to belong and to exist in a meaningful, friendly and hopeful universe. Indeed, the poet Philip Larkin in his verse "Church Going" points out the dilemma left for modern people:

When churches fall completely out of use
What shall we turn them into . . .

. . . superstition, like belief must die
and what remains when disbelief has gone?

14

Grass, weedy pavements, brambles, buttress, sky,
A shape less recognisable every week,
A purpose more obscure.

Yet even for this humanist poet the church meant
something:

A serious house on serious earth it is,
In whose blent air all our compulsions meet,
Are recognised, and robed as destinies.
And that much never can be obsolete,
Since someone will forever be surprising
A hunger in himself to be more serious . . .

Then there is the third aspect in modern life which is
a consequence of secularisation, namely, a PLURALISM OF
VALUE STRUCTURES. Most developed nations now display
a pluralism of values, ideologies and beliefs that would
have been unthinkable two decades ago. Go to any city
or big town in Britain and it will exhibit all the
aspects of a United Nation with every conceivable faith
expressed in its life. No doubt this gives a richness
and excitement which adds a great deal to the quality
of life but it is not without its drawbacks also. The
fundamental problem is that no longer is there to be
found a coherent, value system which the majority affirm
and recognise.

Some years ago, when I was vicar of St Nicholas'
Durham, I was approached by a lecturer at the University and his wife who wished to enrol their children in
the Sunday School and to attend Church, even though
they themselves were agnostics. "Why", I asked, "do you
want your children to hear the Christian message when
you yourselves have rejected it?" Their reply intrigued

and impressed me. They complained about the lack of standards in modern society and affirmed the importance of values and then said "We want our children to grow up in a big 'story'; a story that will give them security, meaning and a hope. It will be their decision later to accept or reject it, but if we do not encourage them to know the Christian 'story' they will never be able to understand what it is they have rejected". This couple went on to express their gratitude for the central role of the Christian story in expressing Christian values as well as forming the marvellous cultural and literary traditions which are central to European and North American culture. "We don't want diminished children", they concluded.

We could easily assume that this gloomy analysis of modern life, in the preceding paragraphs, indicates that western civilisation is irredeemably materialistic and atheistic. However I am not arguing that. What I am suggesting is that our assumptions are materialistic and un-spiritual with the net result that reflection about God and the claims of Jesus Christ have little chance of being considered seriously. The irony however is that modern people are not totally devoid of interest in the supernatural. Indeed not. Somehow this aspect of the human spirit rises to the surface in all kinds of ways. At its most basic level we know of many in our society who, though they do not attend Church regularly, believe in God, pray devoutly, and seem to have a devout awareness of the transcendent. This dimension is not despised or ignored. The behaviour of the many thousands who visit our cathedrals and churches as tourists show that many of them have a residual faith which is stirred by the "signals of the transcendent" which they find in such places.

But then there is the presence in modern society of those who dabble in the occult or astrology, who watch for UFOs, contact spirits, follow the tenets of scientology and other strange groups, practise transcendental meditation, and so on. Those of us who live in the shadow of Glastonbury know only too well the profusion of new faiths and alternative religions which mushroom around here and other such sacred places. All this testifies to the continued pervasiveness of religion. However, most thinking people are put off by the uncritical and superstitious bases of such movements and trends. Nevertheless, the fact of their existence is significant. The American novelist Saul Bellow makes one of his characters say in *Herzog*: "People are dying – it is no metaphor – for lack of something real to carry home when the day is done. See how willingly they accept the wildest nonsense".

Then, of course, there are quasi-religious instincts in us which overlap with faith, and which might coincide with what Philip Larkin meant by being serious about our destinies and compulsions. We can think of art, music, drama and literature which point beyond the mundane and thus feed the souls of people. Often, although not always, the appeal of aesthetics can substitute for what the Christian calls spirituality.

We must also note at civic and national levels the instinctive need felt by authorities to interpret significant events – tragedies, celebrations – religiously. While it is true that churchgoing has declined in recent years in Britain, the interest in the church has not. The Church of England has never enjoyed so much media attention as it has received over the last five years. While there are particular reasons for this attention the fact remains that as western culture has become secularised the issue of faith refuses stubbornly to go away.

First, it refuses to go away at the corporate level. Eisenhower once remarked: "Our government makes no sense unless it is founded in a deeply religious faith – and I don't care what it is!" While that possibly says a great deal about Eisenhower's lack of interest in the character of a faith, he was rightly giving expression to a deep-seated feeling in most of us that if society's values and morality do not spring from an eternal source, that society will be impoverished. The Jewish theologian, J. Neusner, once remarked that "The sense of the transcendent is the heart of culture, the very essence of humanity. A civilisation that is devoted exclusively to the utilitarian is at bottom not different from barbarianism. The world is sustained by unworldliness." We might well say that our God-idea is the acid test of our valuation of life.

Second, it refuses to go away at the personal level. Peter Berger observes in one of his books the resurgence of religion in quarters where one would least expect it and he puts it down to the inability of secular world views to answer the deeper questions of the human condition; questions of whence, whither and why which are ineradicably linked with personhood. He speaks of the "pervasive boredom of a world without gods".

It is crucial then that we start with this background. Unless you and I realize that the world-view we have inherited has made us biased against questions about the supernatural we will not be able to consider the issue of God in a fair-minded way. Without any question we have already been robbed of God by tacit assumptions that only a materialistic world-view makes sense. Hence, most of us have this one-dimensional view of life which does not satisfy the real longings of our hearts. However, in spite of the acids of this form of modernity, many are looking for a vital faith which will bring the whole of them into adjustment with the whole of our relevant experience and which does not ignore the knowledge that has shaped us. Many of us believe that Christianity is that kind of faith.

2

The Case against God

In the last chapter I was suggesting that the climate of modern life has created an atmosphere that has made it very difficult, if not embarrassing, to talk about God in a meaningful way. Talk about politics, sport or current affairs and there will be spirited discussion with people willing to nail their colours to the mast and put their point of view. But talk about God – and there is often a hushed and uncomfortable silence. Of course, we allow him a place in our jokes, and even in important national ceremonies. Religion, it seems, is not a fit topic for civilised people, although curiously most people find it important to give it an important role in dignifying our most solemn ceremonies at private and public moments.

But, to be fair, we cannot attribute the problem completely to modern disregard for matters of faith. The problem is partly created by the facts themselves. Our own experience, as well as the experience of many others, confronts us with serious challenges to the existence of God and forces us to ask, "Is it really possible for intelligent people to believe that a divine, personal Force is responsible for this universe? Is belief in God the final mythology that must go?"

Let us take four issues which are at the heart of modern people's dilemma. For many intelligent people the central problem revolves around our interpretation of life and our experience of it. Two particular issues emerge from this. First, the model of the universe we have inherited is one which comes without a theistic context or theistic values. So, for example, at the level of world history we have imbibed a picture of life as the product of vast impersonal forces which go back millions of years. Countless millions of species have been spawned by an over-generous, even profligate, Nature to fill the world as we know it and in the ensuing history of evolution the weakest and least adaptable forms of life have perished. Entire species have passed away whereas other forms of life have appeared which are destructive and harmful. There may be elements of purpose on a random scale as we look at the whole but there does not seem to be a very caring Providence at work. Thus a new picture of the physical universe and the place of humanity within it has replaced the old cosmology of God at the centre with humanity as his co-regent and partner. And as this picture of life has permeated the corporate mentality of western people, the pattern of our thought has changed with the result that our concept of life, on the whole, is not that of Providence watching over us but is that of an indifferent and uncaring universe which we have to conquer and bring under control.

Along with this assumption, our experience of life either directly, or indirectly through the experiences of others, sometimes leads us to assume that life itself is better explained on the assumption that there is no God rather than that God exists and cares. Where is God, people say, when thousands die suddenly in a volcanic disaster or are swept away in a flood? For some Jews the experience of Auschwitz shattered the concept of a merciful God who cares for his people. The Jewish writer Richard Rubenstein asks, "How can a Jew believe

21

in an omnipotent beneficent God after Auschwitz?" The experience of such evil, he felt, was so overwhelmingly horrible that the whole idea of God had to be revised. We acknowledge that this was not by any means the total Jewish experience because there were many other Jews who did not believe that the character of man's sin should form the agenda for believing in God or not. Nevertheless, even for such devout Jews the question that the Second World War focussed so sharply was, "In the light of such atrocities – where is God?" Thus, the lonely experience of their people during the dark days of the war brought about a major rethink in the Jewish understanding of God.

Although such awful events are outside the experience of most of us we are all aware of the character of human tragedy. We are confronted by it daily as our television sets bring it unannounced into our living rooms. The danger is that this medium can trivialise or even treat it as another element of entertainment. For example, in a recent earthquake in Mexico the television cameras showed the horrifying picture of a trapped little girl of eight who could not be freed from her prison. We could see her head and hear her cries and her prayers – and we heard her die. While it may not have been the intention of the television producer to bring us anything other than news of that awful incident, the superficial quality of the item, programmed to give us instant information, is an example of a tendency to sensationalise rather than inform.

Of course, there is nothing new in this. We are used to reading about tragedy or seeing it happen to others. When, however, it actually happens to us, it ceases to be external and academic and takes on a personal shape. When tragedy hits our own family unit or that of friends, and we have to make sense of the apparently futile happening striking those nearest and dearest to us we find ourselves asking: Where is God when our child is run over or has leukaemia? What kind of God is it who allows these things to happen to us? If he cannot intervene in life when such things happen and when prayer does not seem to work, does it not make more sense to abandon belief in God completely and accept the fact that we are living in a world which is bereft of a loving God, bereft of purpose and meaning? But as we shall see later this conclusion is not inevitable. Somehow belief in a God who cares cannot be shrugged off that easily, the problem of good has to be set against the problem of evil, purposeful events in life against random happenings, morality against immorality, and design against chaos. Nevertheless, the problem of pain and evil remains as the greatest obstacle facing the person who sincerely wants to be a believer. Yet, we have to ask, how much of this problem goes back to a mind-set which has already assumed that God is absent?

A second problem which faces the outsider is that no one these days pretends that we can prove the existence of God from logical argument. Lord Boothby once described God as "that being who exists to have his being proved and disproved", and so it might seem from the development of Christian dogma which has tried to convince people by argument that reason can lead them to God. Take the famous *cosmological argument* so beloved by Thomas Aquinas. This argument is one that depends upon a link between cause and effect. As Thomas saw it everything must have a cause; everything in life comes from potentiality to actuality. Furthermore, there must be a profound similarity between cause and effect, that is, the effect cannot be greater than the cause. Thomas's argument tried to prove that we are led by logic back to a Great Unmoved Mover who was the originating cause of all things. But, philosophically considered, this argument, cogent as it may seem, has two major fallacies. To begin with, why stop at a First Cause? It seems very plausible at first sight that we might be able to trace all of reality back to one Uncaused Event – namely, God Himself. But – why stop at all? Why should there not be an infinite regress of causes and effects?

Then again, Thomas Aquinas argues that the effect cannot be greater than the cause. It is clearly not the case that a cause *has* to be equal to its effects. We know from experience that often something profoundly superior may proceed from the inferior and the history of evolution is an overwhelming testimony to this, proving that the greater does come from the lesser.

The other "proofs" have not fared any better. The argument from design seems at first sight to be very convincing. We see all around us evidence of purpose in creation – that delicate flower, that piece of machinery, the order and rhythm of life – all this and more suggests not a chaotic world but one deliberately planned by a creator. Archdeacon Paley in the last century made this argument famous with his analogy of the world as a clock and God as a purposeful clockmaker who designed an intricate machine and left it to tick away. But as we saw earlier the analogy clearly fails. There is certainly evidence of order and purpose but this does not necessarily indicate that it is the work of a loving Providence. If the world is a clock it certainly does not function as one because there is nothing predictable about the world as a whole or human existence in particular. Disorder flourishes alongside order, the order of cancer creating a world of disorder.

The failure to find a completely convincing argument for God's existence after two thousand years of trying may suggest that it is time to abandon the attempt, throw in the towel and concede that we have made God in our image. God is dead. But Christians are confident that this obituary notice has gone in too early because the idea of God is too persistent to go the way of the Greek mythologies. We shall be returning to the question of proofs, or "clues" as I prefer to call them, later but two things can be said immediately to the cry, "Let's abandon faith in God". Firstly, logical proof is necessarily limited to a range of things where the answer is already included in the data. We call this *a priori* reasoning because the argument proceeds from data before us. For example, the answer to 144 multiplied by 145 is found by deduction from what is already implicit in numbers. *A priori* reasoning has a most important place in life, especially where mathematics form the basis of science. But how limited this pathway of knowledge really is, in spite of its importance. Just think how splendid it would be if the most complex questions of life could be solved that simply. Think of political issues to do with human freedom, economic justice, male/female and black/white relationships. How convenient it would be if everyone could agree about the conclusion to be reached! But experience shows that life does not come in that form and shape and most of our genuine "knowing" has more than just a whiff of speculation about it.

A personal illustration might help to bring this home.

The Great God Robbery

After twenty-eight years of happy marriage to a truly
magnificent person who has fulfilled all the hopes I have
rested in her, I still cannot prove that she loves me. I have
plenty of clues, of course, but no direct, tangible proof
which would satisfy the objective outsider who, perhaps,
had to make up his mind in a few hours. Suppose in that
brief period he caught us having an argument! Would
that not act as a serious objection to the flimsy statement
that "She loves me"? Again, even in the best of relationships there have been the bad moments, the times when
cruel things have been said and mischief planned. Do we
not have to take these into the reckoning? Yes, indeed, we
must and they are important clues concerning the nature
of human knowing because love grows from disappointment and conflict. Love cannot be proved because there
is always a great open-endedness about it and to say "she
loves me" implies a strong element of faith. That does
not mean that one cannot say "she loves me". Indeed,
we can say that and much more; that this kind of love
is far superior to any form of love which can be proved
by deductive reasoning, because of necessity that which
is measurable is bound to be superficial and very limited,
whereas the experience of love forged over many years
will deepen and continue to grow forever. So Professor
J. Baillie comments: "A high degree of probability is
the most that can be claimed for any scientific result.
Yet, the strange fact is that I have more confidence in
what common sense and pre-scientific experience tell
me about my natural environment than in any of the
things I have learned from science. I have, for example,
a greater degree of assurance of the honesty and loyalty
of some of my friends than I have of the validity of any
scientific doctrine and still more secure is my conviction

that honesty and loyalty are things required of us."

The second observation is that attempting to prove God says a great deal about our concept of God and our understanding of ourselves. We make him into an element of knowledge "out there" and our implicit thinking is that "if only we had the right receiving equipment we could hear him speaking to us". I have no wish to deny the fact that God is outside of us in a real sense, but such space-time concepts are manifestly anthropocentric. In a profound way we have to take on board that if there is a God we are "inside" him. He is not "out there" as if he is a statistic, fact or piece of knowledge. Rather, if he is the God of Christian theology he is the whole of knowledge – and he will therefore be ultimately beyond knowledge unless he chooses to reveal himself. Because of him, knowing and knowledge are possible and we exist.

But for the moment we must stay with the fact that the Christian Church has given up the attempt to prove the existence of God. He cannot be measured or confined according to the patterns of our ways and modern theologians have wisely refused to be drawn.

A third objection to God is closely linked with the problem of meaning. When Christians talk abut God, surely, we might think, their words should have the same meaning as when they are used in day by day life. Here we meet the problem of logic and common sense meanings. Centuries ago Augustine focussed upon the problem when he posed the issue in this way, that the presence of evil in the world implies that either God is good and yet limited in some way, or that he is powerful but not good. It seemed to Augustine in his pre-Christian days that he could not be both. In theological language this meant that his omnipotence and his beneficence were in conflict. If he were good and powerful, then it seemed that he would intervene on behalf of the poor and helpless. The fact that he doesn't seems to indicate that we have to make a choice. Of course, as Augustine was to see later as a Christian, there are factors that we have to take into account that diminish this actual problem. For example, perhaps God has a plan which takes into account all the world's sufferings and evils. Again, the simple either/or may be making the assumption that it is this world's cares that matter. But if God has prepared for those who love him such a wealth of joy and happiness which dwarfs the brief and transitory pains of earth (no matter how awful they may seem to us) does not this put the whole issue in a completely different context? In other words, when we talk in terms of either omnipotence or goodness but not both, we are smuggling in a value system which has its own inbuilt assumption that if God exists he must exist to make us all happy in this life.

However, although we have to be very cautious when we use this argument we have to acknowledge that if words mean anything at all it is sometimes very difficult to talk about God being good when things happen which contradict our understanding of what a good friend would do for us. For example, if I tell a young lady that she is beautiful, graceful and intelligent and in the same breath add, "but it is a pity you are so awkward, a little thick and 100 pounds overweight" – she will be very puzzled, as well as very annoyed! The point is that the additional statement has shattered the earlier idea with which we started. Now, of course, this is obvious when we use ordinary language but if words are to carry their normal values we become aware of the problems when we speak about God as good. At the moment of writing this chapter I am dealing with an intelligent couple whose eleven year old son died very inexplicably during a sports afternoon at school. They have no church connections whatever. So how do I interpret for them the activity of God in this situation? How can I tell them that in spite of what they are experiencing God actually loves them and cares for them and he has taken their son to himself? Now I happen to believe that is the case, but my confidence rests on many years of working things out theologically as a Christian. It is not possible that those outside the Christian family can see it in the same way, because it is clearly not good for them and certainly not meaningful if that word has any reality.

Thus the Christian or any theist struggles with language when she is trying to convey something of the meaning of God for others. Christian thinkers find help in referring to analogy when we talk about God. It is clear, for example, that when we try to talk about any deep reality which is beyond space or time that we will be forced into metaphors, pictures and analogies. Listen to Gerard Hopkins trying to convey something of the splendour of creation:

> The world is charged with the grandeur of God
> It will shine forth as shining from shot foil

Watch any film of a literary masterpiece and you will see the inability of the screen to express real emotion or the depth of human expression. Some things are beyond words and we hopelessly resort to pictures. Science itself is not immune from this. Popularisers of science have not hesitated to use diagrams, metaphors and concepts to portray realities which are beyond the reach of human words. Indeed, modern quantum physicists are not afraid to use metaphor and poetry to describe the realities that are their concern.

A fourth problem for the sincere person who would like to believe but finds it difficult is located in the idea of belief itself. Such a person might put it this way: "I'd actually like to believe but find the whole concept of worship rather puzzling. I don't think I need God to find my way in life. I cope very well, I enjoy the finer things of life, beauty, art and music, and find genuine pleasure in these things. Frankly, Church bores me. It is not that I hate the service, the people or even the vicar! It is just that it is not for me." I think we have to heed this kind of statement very seriously. There are people who, to quote Karl Rahner, are "unmusical in religion". That is to say, those who do not appear to pick up the sounds which other people hear and we have to admit that there are plenty of them around – in our family circle, at work and among our friends. For such people who appear to get by happily without the God hypothesis, what has faith to say to them? Is God only useful as a support for church attendance and for those who conform to the practices of established religion? I only hope that those who are "unmusical" in such matters to do with organised Christianity will be concerned with the central matter of belief. If our enquiry leads us to the conclusion that God exists and has appeared in and through the ministry of Jesus Christ, the logic will lead us on to doing something about it.

For some, like Erich Fromm, the great psychiatrist, the problem is linked with the thrust of a faith. He criticises Christianity in particular because it appears to address its message mainly to weak people. He agrees that it is very successful in helping the weak and needy but he asserts that if it is to be successful in the modern world it must have a message for strong people, people who do not have problems, people who are successful in life and who can cope. What, asks Fromm, is your message to people like me who are happy, contented and balanced? Bonhoeffer, of course, addressed a similar question before his untimely death. The world has come of age, he thought, and does not need the religion of former times. How can the Church minister in a religionless age? What is its message to those who not only appear not to need it but actually despise it?

But a curious illogicality runs through this argument. What has need to do with it? We all recognise that there are those who do not feel any particular religious need. Perhaps most of us are like that and this is a question that we shall return to later. And Fromm's argument that Christianity is more attractive to weak than to strong people is certainly highly contentious! What is the case is that more people choose not to go to church because they have other interests than because they have logically come to the conclusion that God does not exist. Need, is NOT the issue – truth is. If God *is*, then our unmusicality in religion is neither here nor there. If he is the Lord of the universe then I stand before him as a child of the universe and must work out what this relationship now means and what I must do about it.

3

Is the Universe on Our Side?

A very interesting shift in our thinking has taken place since man set foot on the moon. Although Copernicus, years ago, destroyed the idea that the sun and stars revolve around the earth, an earth-bound approach to life was practically impossible to shift because our experience of life was confined to the limits of our knowledge here. But since 1969 a wholly new consciousness of the universe has begun to filter into the experience of us all; as a result of which we have begun to be conscious of our place in the universe and not merely in our world. We are now used to seeing the earth from satellite pictures with the vast spaces of the universe behind. Furthermore, the signals being transmitted to us from our space ships, interviewing the nearest planets, increase our new sense of awareness of being children of a universe which dwarfs our tiny world.

Now, how do we react to this? Our response can take one of two main forms. First, we may be excited and awed by this realisation. We now know so much more about the universe than before and its very size frankly makes comprehension of it extremely difficult. How can we possibly absorb the fact that, as far as we can tell, the universe consists of innumerable galaxies like our own; the nearest one to us being 900,000 light years away! Yet, although we are dwarfed by the immensity of all that is, the nature of our humanity comes out in our desire to understand and inhabit the cold confines of limitless space. We want to know and we respond eagerly to the challenge. We project our thoughts beyond ourselves and ask whether perhaps there are other species like us out there inhabiting worlds similar to our own. Is it conceivable that we are a unique offshoot of Mother Nature? Is ours the only world in the entire universe where there is conscious life?

A common assumption today is that our planet cannot be unique; there must exist somewhere in the universe sentient, thinking beings with whom we shall eventually make contact. But at the moment this remains a matter of faith because no evidence whatsoever has come to light to substantiate that theory, only the odds that we cannot be a freak. Given similar conditions in a similar world, it is likely, so we are told, that similar beings exist somewhere. This conclusion I have no wish to dispute. That may well be so. Given the disastrous mess that humanity has made of God's world it is at least possible that God could be trying other experiments elsewhere! What we cannot doubt, however, is that our new sense of the universe has challenged our thinking concerning the nature of God himself. No longer is it possible to think of God in domestic terms. He is, if he exists, a being who cannot be adequately caught by the workings of the human mind, who is wholly other and only knowable in so far as he reveals himself to us.

A second response, beside that of awe which leads to intellectual curiosity, is that of sheer metaphysical numbness when one begins to comprehend the nature of the universe. Here is the start of existential doubt. Consider the psychological effect of this piece of information. We are told that the light from the cluster of galaxies in

Hydra which reach us, have travelled through space for two thousand million light years. That cluster is only one of innumerable galaxies, each made up of millions of stars, separated from each other by immeasurable stretches of inter-galactic space. Ponder this picture of the universe and then ask: "What do I mean when I say God?" How much closer seems the domestic God of the Bible who made the heavens and the earth! Here then we meet another part of the "Great God Robbery" that the size of the universe terrifies us and seems to place beyond our reach a God who cares. We find ourselves thinking: "All this is so vast that if there is a God he cannot possibly be interested in the antics of a tiny species on a third rate planet orbiting a tenth-rate sun". It is against this realistic background that we wonder: "Is the universe for us or against us? Are we but aliens in a foreign world, strange dwellers in a world that will never be ours?"

Of course from one point of view we are not strangers. We are products of nature and inherit its riches. We may pride ourselves on being projected to a position of ascendancy over all things in our world but the common cold pricks the bubble of our conceit. Rulers we may be but still subject to nature's laws. Indeed, there are many who entreat us to be content with our lot as nothing but nature's offspring. "You can do nothing to alter what already is", they scold us. "Enjoy what you have got and do not hanker after the unattainable. Mortal you are – make the most of it." But how inadequate such advice is because the one thing we cannot be is content with this world. Why is it that of all creatures, only humankind find this restless urge to reach beyond ourselves? We do not feel at home in this world. It offers much but its best delights are tarnished with impermanence and disappointment. The history of humanity is a biography of our search for fulfilment. Hope projects humanity forward in a never-ending quest for self-discovery in art, music, scientific discovery and, perhaps most revealingly of all, in a diverse religious search. There in a thirst for the eternal we stand revealed as spiritual beings reaching out to understand and to be understood. Does the universe give us any clues concerning this quest? Are we alone or do we indeed have a "cosmic friend" as R. W. Sellars once put it?

I think that our starting point must be with the character of the world as we find it. Yes, we do find it alien to us at many points but there is a greatly overlooked aspect of creation which yields a most interesting point. The area I am concerned with now is the fact that deeply imbedded in its structure and existence is the fact of rationality. That is, the fact that I can reason, know and make conclusions is not only something to do with me but more importantly with the world I live in. Humankind may pat itself on the back for creating a network of intelligent structures and thus imposing an orderly framework for us to enjoy life but the greatly overlooked fact is that we could only do this because the intelligence was implicitly there. That is to say, that at the heart of this highly complex and diverse universe an inherent rationality resides which is the origin of all creativity. We have only been able to make our wheels, build our ships, cars and planes, design and make our computers – and so on – because the structure of things has been conducive to such progress. Science is only possible because we live in an ordered universe which complies with mathematical laws. So Peter Berger notes: "Yet the most astounding result of modern natural science is the reiterated discovery that nature, too, is in its essence a fabric of mathematical relations. Put crudely, the mathematics that man projects out of his own consciousness somehow corresponds to the mathematical reality that is external to him and which indeed his consciousness appears to reflect."

Such is our conviction concerning this that we have no hesitation in assuming that this applies to every part of the universe, whether we have been there or not, because our experience is of the universe as a vast material system, the fundamental particles of which interact according to general laws. Once we begin to think about it, it must strike us all as an astonishing fact. We took it all for granted at school. Our textbooks on physics, biology and chemistry opened to us a world in which we are able to study the principles which govern the patterns of life and also predict how things behave.

The kind of order I am thinking of might be best illustrated by an analogy. Let us suppose a traveller in visiting a foreign land finds himself entering a deserted house in a wilderness. He is struck by the fact that although there is no sign of the presence of another person there are signs that someone has been there before him. He deduces this by the fact that everything in the house is sufficient for his survival. To be sure, not everything is ready-made or fully prepared but all the ingredients are there, everything works in a clocklike way. So he concludes that the evidence of order indicates that the house has had an owner and it could be that he is still around. He could have come to another conclusion, of course. He might have decided that it only seems to suggest order and the likeliest hypothesis is that it is an amazing coincidence to find in the wilderness a place of such convenience. He might also have concluded that in spite of many opportunities, the former occupant has never showed up; thus proving that the house was just a freak happening. However, the more order he finds in the house, discovering that he and his descendants are able to grow within it and never tire of new discoveries to meet the needs of new situations, may lead to the conclusion that the hypothesis that it happened by chance is unconvincing.

We recognise the deficiency of all analogies but I am suggesting that the fact of such striking implicit intelligence and temporal order forces us to give an account of it. Now when you and I use our technology in day to day working situations we can adopt at least three different attitudes to the fact of such inherent rationality. The first is that we can take it all for granted. It is there. This is the most common attitude in our society. The fact that the world is rational is a brute fact and it neither proves the existence of God nor disproves it. Sadly, when we did science at school few of our teachers opened our eyes to the wonder of all around us. We were never taught to ask "Why?", but simply taught that "It exists" without any explanation given. But science without wonder leads to the impoverishment of the human spirit, and can result in a Philistine stance to life which exploits the goodness of life and does not apprehend the Goodness in life.

A second and probably more common attitude among thinking people if asked to say something about the presence of rationality in the nature of things, would probably be that rationality is a concept we impose upon the world. "It simply is not the case that raw data is rational", says a sympathetic but agnostic friend. "All that we find in life are the building blocks of scientific discovery and when some order is found we project back into the data the concept of rationality! If you are going on to say that this 'proves' the existence of God, it does nothing of the sort. All it shows is that you have made an unwarranted jump from 'Things make sense' to 'It is God who makes them sensible'." So our friend attempts to pour cold water upon the concept of the universe as basically intelligible. For him rationality resides in us and not in the world around and its structures. All we are able to say is that the character of the world is such that it has produced intelligent beings. Nothing more can or ought to be said than this.

I respond very seriously to the thrust of the last point. It is very tempting for the Christian believer to say, "Didn't I tell you that this proves the existence of God? Open your eyes and see his handiwork all around us!" But this is not what I am arguing. Instead I would assert that we can say a lot more than that the character of the world just happens to have produced sentient, intelligent beings. The point I am trying to make as strongly as possible is that the element of intelligibility is not something that we impose on things after we have created something, but it is already there in our environment as well as in ourselves. The world is either intelligible or not; if it is not, science is impossible because the world would be haphazard and chaotic. But that is not our experience; rather it is predictable and orderly. I am not arguing that a mysterious purpose called "God" is somehow present in that inanimate piece of steel that will eventually become a car chassis or the wool that will become a jumper. Of course not. But we are only able to make these things because there is a basic irretrievable "givenness" about the world and our place in it which has propelled humanity from a primitive home in the seas or the trees (whichever theory of evolution one takes) to the limitless possibilities which still exist before us – assuming that our predilection to self destruction does not lead to a final act of total genocide.

The point I have just been making is that the world as it is – with all the ready-made ingredients for intelligent life, thus making possible the wonder of science, art and human growth and development – requires an explanation. Now it could be countered by someone saying, "Yes. I can see why a theist believes in God on this basis. I grant you that the order and signs of intelligence are there and this makes all our knowledge possible. But what if it all depends upon an initial act of complete random chance? What if the creation of the universe is but the inevitable outcome of a series of accidents at the beginning of time? If that were the case we would not conclude that the order indicates the presence of intelligent activity on the part of a divine being we call 'God' but, rather, the order is but the manifestation of structural order which keeps the Cosmos going." Some have illustrated this by saying that although a monkey could not produce the complete works of Shakespeare, it is conceivable that three thousand monkeys typing for two thousand years would eventually yield this result at some point in time. This idea is as improbable as a similar sentiment expressed in the limerick:

There was once a hairy baboon
Who breathed down a bassoon.
For he said: "It appears,
in a billion years –
I shall certainly hit on a tune".

But this idea that instinctive reaction working itself out over millions of years can burst forth into brilliant creativity is most certainly nonsense. Irrationality cannot give rise to rationality in that kind of form. For the sake of argument let us accept the unlikely idea that haphazard blowings by a baboon may hit upon the *Trumpet Voluntary*, but even accepting that the law of averages states it might happen, such a mindless discovery of a tune falls a long way short of the rational, purposeful, creative mind which composed the tune in the first place.

If, then, we can say cautiously that it is reasonable to conclude that the impressive order in the universe might be the work of a personal Intelligence we seem to be in a position to wonder whether there is any other evidence to believe in the existence of a Creator?

Let us now go back to the problem of "Someone who started it all". This, actually, is our gut-reaction. You ask the average person and you will find that most people find the cause and effect argument a reasonable ground for believing in God. "There must be a God who created all this", is a common assumption. This should not be dismissed as hopeful credulity because often it is said by people who are not practising Christians at all. Many are students of life whose conviction stems not from analytical thinking in a study but from a lifetime's reflection on the character of life and the beauty of creation.

Nevertheless, as we have seen the cause and effect argument is not without its difficulties. That *d* is the result of *c*, which is the result of *b* which is the result of *a*, is all very obvious. But the statement that *a* is the beginning of the series requires an explanation. Why stop there? Is *a* the logical origin of *b*, thus causing *c* and *d*? If not, perhaps *a* itself is caused? This is the basic difficulty with the famous First Cause argument as propounded by Aquinas. We can happily accept that we can trace back the steps into the past but why is it necessary to introduce God as the ultimate cause of it all? Why not an infinite regress as was suggested earlier?

It seems then that the First Cause argument is badly holed by a logical flaw but, interestingly, this ancient argument has reappeared somewhat strengthened by two considerations. The first has to do with recent cosmological theories. It is now commonly believed that the universe had a beginning in time. As long as Hoyle's steady state theory prevailed, which argued that the universe has always existed in a state of perfect equilibrium, the First Cause argument was bound to be unfashionable. However, this theory has since given way to discoveries in radio astronomy which suggest that in one wholly inexplicable explosion the universe began its life. It has been possible to date the origin of the universe to an explosion which occurred about eighteen million years ago. Two particular arguments bolster the theory that the universe is finite. The first is the second law of thermodynamics which, as one of the universal laws of life, simply explains the process of life and death. Order is always followed by disorder; life by death. Scientists conclude from this that if, as is likely, the universe is moving towards its own decay and death, the conclusion is that it must be a finite universe and did not always exist. The second reason is that the American astronomer, Edwin Hubble, discovered that galaxies, instead of remaining in a stable condition, were in fact rushing apart. This discovery was to prove decisive. Radio astronomy has verified this hypothesis of the expanding universe which again supports the idea of a universe which had a beginning in time. We are also told that all the ingredients for life were encoded within the first ten seconds of the beginning of the universe. Little wonder that Dr Schwiama's lecture on the Origin of Life on Radio Three commenced with the announcer saying, "Professor Schwiama will not be saying anything about the supernatural beginnings of the universe as the natural beginnings are strange enough!"

It is important that we should not fall back into the "God of the gaps" syndrome which tries to fit God into things we cannot explain. Even a superficial knowledge of the facts surrounding the origin of life and the new information brought to us through radio astronomy will convince us all that it is unwise to come to trite and simplistic conclusions. However this is not my intention. Instead, I wish to point out what the implications might be. Since it is widely agreed that the universe had a beginning we can assume that the universe could not have caused itself. It must have been caused by something or someone else who is outside.

Professor P. Davies resists this argument. In a recent book he writes: "When giving lectures on cosmology I am often asked what happened before the big bang. The answer, that there was no 'before', is regarded with suspicion. But cause and effect are temporal concepts and cannot be applied to a state in which time does not exist;

42

the question is meaningless". But Professor Davies's conclusion is not irresistible, even given the theory that space and time concepts belong to the conditions of this universe. The moment we agree that the universe is finite in duration includes within it the conclusion that something was created from nothing. Professor Davies has unfortunately fudged the issue in ducking an obvious question. As a scientist he is reluctant to be drawn away from the data before him but philosophically the fact that something is created from nothing and continues to be cries out to be answered. This, in essence, is classical Christian teaching; that *ex nihilo* God created. But at this point we have to recognise that that deduction has moved beyond the evidence. That the universe had a beginning in time possibly only proves that it was caused, not that "God" caused it because there is nothing in the data to give us any information regarding the character or the identity of the Causer. Only revelation can give us that information. Nevertheless, it is arguably the case that the existence of an eternal being, the uncreated creator, provides an answer for the question: "Who started it?"

The further reason why the "First Cause" argument has returned to favour is because thinkers have started to look at the issue not simply from the perspective of cause and effect but as well from the fact that the universe is a reality and has to be accounted for. Now this is something we are told we should not do. We are told you cannot move from details in the world to ultimate questions about the universe because there is no identity whatever between the two sets of questions. It's like moving from Aunt Betty's knitting to the Presidency of the United States. But why should not the question of the existence of a divine Creator be treated seriously as a proper question? If astronomers and others can speculate seriously about the possibility of thinking beings, similar to ourselves, existing somewhere in the universe, on the basis of no firm evidence, can we not make intelligent deductions about the creation of the universe based more firmly upon our knowledge of our world? A very important book published recently by the Cambridge physicist Dr Stephen Hawking entitled *A Brief History of Time* argues that the presence of life may point to an act of God although he is at pains to explore alternatives. This theory is called the "Anthropic principle" which relies upon very precise calculations about the probability that life forms would eventually emerge somewhere in the universe. He writes: "The initial rate of expansion would have to be chosen very precisely for the rate of expansion still to be so close to the critical rate needed to avoid recollapse. This means that the initial state of the universe must have been chosen very carefully indeed if the hot big bang model was correct right back to the beginning of time. It would be very difficult to explain why the universe should have begun in just this way, except as the act of God who intended to create beings like us."

But is it right to make the quantum leap from things within our experience to that without? Why not be content with agnosticism and allow that we shall never know the answer to questions which lurk beyond our world of space and time. I want to argue that it is quite proper for us to ask these questions even though we are prepared to come up against the limits of our knowledge. This, we suggest, is far better than succumbing to the robbery of a culture which has already closed its mind. The question, then, "why does this universe exist at all?" is a proper question because it arises from our perception that things do not generally just happen. There are reasons why things occur and the possibility that the universe was caused by something or someone who stands in a personal relationship with all created things is not something we can just dismiss. The striking fact that the present state of play in astronomical research is leading to the exploration of cosmological theories encourages us to believe that our quest is far from ill-conceived or stupid.

We therefore conclude this section by stating that the "God" hypothesis is not as wild and as improbable as some have claimed. The existence of all that is fairly cries out for an explanation and the striking intelligibility of creation suggests the probability of an intelligent mind behind all the things that are. The Princeton physicist Professor Freeman Dyson stated in a BBC broadcast: "I do feel like an alien in the universe. The more I study the details of its architecture the more evidence I find that the universe in some sense must have known that we were coming."

4

A Personal Creator?

In the last chapter we were thinking about the signs of rationality in the world which gives rise to the conviction that God exists. We saw that there is in humanity a somewhat innate feeling or possibly even an assumption that "someone" is behind all this. Our agnostic friends sometimes tell us that they have difficulty believing in God but we remind them that not believing in God may possibly be a more problematical undertaking. When experts can show us with models of electrons and neutrons how it was possible for the big bang to occur spontaneously out of nothing, we find ourselves asking, "But how, philosophically, can anything occur out of nothing? In the light of the fact that we are inescapably part and parcel of the world and universe, is it not possible that the conscious and intelligent life we possess is not simply an extraordinary accident but actually reflects the nature of creation?"

For those who are young at heart Walt Disney's wonderful film *Love Bug* is an enjoyable feast of escapism. It is the story of a Volkswagen car which is discovered to have a strange personal identity. Odd things happen when people drive it; it takes off by itself and appears to know what people are saying of it even though it cannot communicate directly with them. Its devoted mechanic bursts out at one point: "It isn't just a bundle of parts, sprockets, pistons and gears – it's Herbie!" Of course, nobody seriously watches films like that believing that a mechanical thing can think, make logical decisions and have emotions, but as I watched it again quite recently I found myself asking what do we mean by such words as "person", "personality", "mind" and, especially, "consciousness". To be a person, we are all agreed, is to have a conscious will and to be able to form rational opinions and make decisions. This is what Herbie was supposed to have and this idea – so improbable – gave to the film its hilarious character.

The question of consciousness raises the issue of the boundary between mind and matter as well as the fundamental disagreement between the believer in God and the materialist. The materialistic position assumes that everything in creation is reducible to material elements; there is nothing which cannot be explained in scientific terms. We must leave to one side many of the elements in this long-standing argument and concentrate instead on the problem of what we mean by consciousness. The more we consider it, the more mysterious it appears to be. Let us consider, for example, our experience of thought. On the one hand, I can have thoughts which are obviously connected to human needs and desires. "How I am looking forward to that steak and chips tonight!", we might find ourselves thinking. Such reactions lend support to the materialist argument of the connection between the physical and mental. But at other times, as I write, and as you read, our minds are full of abstract ideas which appear to have little connection with material things. We find our minds soaring above physical desires and reaching towards a realm of "being" where we feel naturally at home. For this reason, it has long been the opinion of thinkers down the centuries that the existence of "mind" is an obvious proof of God. John Locke, the English philosopher, wrote: "If then there must be something eternal, let us see what sort of being it must be. It is very obvious to reason that it must necessarily be a cogitative being. For it is as impossible to conceive, that ever bare incogitative matter should produce a thinking intelligent being, as that nothing should of itself produce matter."

There are strengths and weaknesses with Locke's argument. The weaknesses are twofold; philosophical and physical. The philosophical problems start with Locke's assumption that the incogitative matter cannot produce intelligence. That may be the case, a philosopher friend will tell us, but it does not follow logically. It might possibly be the case that inanimate things may reach a state of development when consciousness begins. The evolutionary record shows that highly-developed species have emerged from more primitive forms of life – at the very least we must acknowledge that possibility. The physical problem with Locke's assertion is that we know for a fact that there is a direct link between brain events and mental events. A blow on the head may lead to the loss of consciousness or memory, or something more serious may result. Damage to the physical brain can have an affect on speech and even more terribly lead to mental derangement and loss of personal identity. We all know of people who through senile dementia have deteriorated tragically. The clear evidence is that there is a link between the brain and consciousness whether this is causal or not.

It would seem then that Locke's argument is fatally damaged by the way the physical brain is affected by material events and by the way it in turn affects what we call the mind. But this would be a superficial judgement because the case that they are identical has not been proved. Indeed, this is where Locke's argument is strong and where extreme materialism is very weak. For the materialist, consciousness is the accidental epiphenomenon of the brain's activity. That is to say, thought at every level is an immediate result of brain states. Some have concluded that as the terms are virtually synonymous they talk of the "mind-brain". But the invention of an unattractive new word does not solve an old problem. Is it in fact the case that we have to yield the ground to the materialist and confess that there is no reality to the mind – it is but the word we give to neural activity in our brains?

Now, we have already accepted that a neural connection exists between brain and mind. I am not suggesting that when I think of a brilliant idea and cry "Eureka" that this has been done independently of my brain by a ghost-like "mind" which lives somewhere within me. Of course not. That complex computer which we call the human brain is obviously being pulled into service when we argue, think, contemplate and decide. But it is being pulled into service and not doing it all by itself! Roger Sperry, the neuro-psychologist who discovered the differential functions of the brain's cerebral hemispheres, has directly contradicted the reductionists who argue that the consciousness is nothing more than the outcome of psychological events in the body. He points to the extreme unlikelihood of non-mental functions creating mental activities (and thus, independently, supports Locke's argument mentioned earlier) and he argues for a directive principle in us which is rational and conscious. He states that "mind is that which moves matter in the brain". That is to say, without denying the mind-body relationship, he rejects a materialistic basis for conscious thought as an inadequate explanation of the complex brain-mind relationship. Human choosing, of course, lends us many useful illustrations of the way the purely physical side of life may be dominated by higher principles. Let us take but just one. We all know the tremendously strong pull in us all to survive. It is natural to shrink from pain, violence and extreme danger. But how often we hear stories of people who have done heroic acts in the face of this natural instinct for survival as, for example, when a person flings himself in front of a terrorist in order to save another human being. Such overtly "irrational" behaviour (in the sense that it is not in our own interest to do this) can only be explained by altruistic motives shaped by ideas of love, justice and God which are beyond the reach of the purely physical. Somehow, there is something profoundly human in such choosing which cannot be classified under a materialistic category. Our mental experience of abstract and pure thought mocks a simplistic identification between such happenings and neurological states. We all are aware of ourselves as persons who, while having physical emotions, bodily experiences, sensations, and mental events, cannot be limited to just one set of them. Our consciousness of life and the way cerebral thought has shaped the world places us over and against nature in some ways, as well as within it.

What then do we make of the connection between the brain and the conscious mind? Are we faced with a dualism of mind and body? This cannot be, and for some of the reasons given above would be unacceptable. When we think of the powerful mind of Einstein, or the brilliance of Shakespeare, or the intuition, commitment and scholarship of Madame Curie we find ourselves rejecting the notion that all such activity is nothing more than an intricate network of nerve endings and pulsating electrical currents. No doubt such elements are included in the process but it is surely not enough to convey the reality of mind in our experience and life in general. No – what we might postulate is the strong possibility of a directive conscious intelligence which is given to us as human beings and which separates us from the rest of the animal kingdom.

With whom then do we share this quality or faculty? The answer we have the temerity to suggest is that this quality of conscious life is not a freak event which just happened to occur to a certain species but, rather, is something which links us with the heart of the universe. This consciousness is also personal, which of course Herbie could never be!

But it is proper to ask a further question at this point. "Do we really have evidence that there is a directive and intelligent principle in the universe?" It hardly seems so when we take into account some of the problems we glanced at in chapter two. However, when we talk about intelligence two things spring immediately to mind; purpose and design. When a fashion designer is creating his or her Autumn Collection these two principles are obviously central. The purpose may have beauty and elegance as the primary objectives with warmth probably as a very poor third. The "creator" purposes to arrive at an article which expresses his image of gracefulness. Indeed, the use of the word creation, so frequently used by fashion designers, reveals the intention to innovate in a wholly revolutionary way. The design, we might say, is the outworking of the scheme, as a beautiful gown is created and eventually modelled. That intelligence is at work in dress design is sometimes questioned mischievously by some of us, but no doubt to those who are the purchasers, it is all self-evident. They are convinced that a brilliant and creative mind has caught hold of their needs.

When this kind of argument is translated into the quest to find purpose and intelligence in creation generally it is sometimes called the teleological argument after the Greek word *telos* meaning "goal" or "end". So, we have to ask: "Are there clear evidences in life that a conscious, intelligent Principle behind all the things that are, designed this puzzling universe?" The evidence cannot be said to be conclusive. On the one hand there appear to be clear signs of purpose. No one can deny them. We find it in nature as well as in human life. In nature life works uniformly to plans encoded in the genetic code of a plant or animal. Things grow according to their kind. There is a wonderful beauty and symmetry about the order of creation. As we saw in the last chapter the scientist working in his laboratory cannot do his work without this as a basic datum of research. This givenness of purpose gives life its meaning and has led to humanity attaining the level of civilisation which we now enjoy.

But, we have to say again, who can deny the existence of those elements which appear to refute the idea that there is a personal intelligence behind all living things. Take the apparent randomness of creative life. It hardly seems possible that a benign creator is behind the tortuous fortunes and misfortunes of evolution in which savagery, disease and wantonness seem to be the shape of things. When we consider the undoubted order of life we pause when we meet the terrible order of cancer division or the volcanic disaster which destroys the lives of thousands. "God be praised!" say the devout parents of a teenager rescued from that volcanic eruption. "God's will be done" pray the bereaved parents of another teenager killed in the same disaster. But where is God in it all? Surely, says the sceptic, the evidence all around us compels us to believe that there is no such thing as a personal intelligence behind all things. Our experience of such terrible acts seems to contradict the hypothesis of a loving creator. So, some people conclude, all we need say is that life needs order for there to be life and this creates the illusion that a rational being stands behind it all.

This point does seem very plausible until one considers the fact that order outweighs disorder in the scheme of things. Indeed, the history of creation reveals the outworking of purpose (even if, for the moment, we desist in surmising whether that is personal or blind) as the movement from the primitive to more advanced forms of life proceeds steadily onwards. Of course there are facts in creation which seem to contradict the notion of an intelligent purpose behind the universe but in noting these at this point we should not minimise the existence of the good, the glorious and the beautiful which dominate the created order.

When we consider the fact of *design* the same ambivalent picture appears and it is not my intention to *prove* the existence of God from such evidences of design that I may be able to extract from creation. It may be recalled that Archdeacon Paley attempted to prove the existence of God from design. He was convinced that the world showed clear signs of purposeful creation and argued that nature's design greatly surpasses human ingenuity in art, science and human thought. He argued that if one found a watch on a moor one would not assume that the watch came there by chance but one would reasonably deduce that a watchmaker existed somewhere. So, he said, the universe is very much like a watch. We find many things in it which seem to be made up of parts which work together to achieve a certain goal. Just as we reason the existence of a watchmaker from the watch so we might fairly assume the existence of a personal Deity from the existence of the universe.

There is a rather fatal flaw in Paley's argument which is simply that the relationship between a watch found on a moor and the universe is hardly an identical one. The observer is outside the first but inside the second. I mean by this, that when I argue from watches to other events in the natural world I am the observer of an article which I know has been fashioned by human intelligence. In the case of the universe my position as an observer is different. I am more like a goldfish in a bowl, speculating if anything exists outside my bowl – even if there is a bowl! This weakens greatly the force of the argument. It is clear then that the starting point is going to be very different.

A second problem is that it seems that Paley has smuggled into his argument categories which are questionable. As I pointed out above, the person who finds the watch has already encountered watches before and that is why he is able to say that it has been designed by a person. So J. S. Mill commented, "If I found a watch on a moor I should infer that it had been left by a human being. The inference would not be for design but because I know that watches are made by men." So it looks as though Paley has innocently introduced confusion by supposing that there is some correlation between a watch and the world around. The first is known to us because it is created by human workmanship; the other dwarfs us by its immensity and mystery.

Indeed, Paley's argument seemed to meet its doom once and for all when Darwin's theory of Natural Selection appeared, which seemed to argue so persuasively that design is brought about not by a personal Intelligence behind all things but by natural factors which favoured the development of certain species which arose by chance.

But Paley's argument does in fact present some useful points and it has recently come back into favour and we must consider the reason why. For a start it is now well known that Darwin's theory of Natural Selection is not exactly what he claimed for it. It is not as chanceless and as random as he supposed. Running through the stream of evolution is a family likeness which links parents to offspring in each generation. It is sometimes said of a new baby that he is a "chip off the old block" or "how like his mother". We expect to find differences which enshrine originality, of course, but it is usually set in the continuity between parent and child. This steady identity is as important for the continuation of the species as are the variations which introduce the new. It is possible then to hold that the general shape of Paley's theory may still be maintained because it is concerned about that purposiveness which suggests the activity of a personal God. As F. R. Tennant so trenchantly put it: "the survival of the fittest presupposes the arrival of the fit". We can accept, then, Paley's basic argument that the world provides many examples of happenings geared to goals and to certain ends. Eyes function in order for people to see – and not the other way round. Professor C. A. Coulson used to say that very few scientists can avoid the language of teleology because of the principle of order latent in the very nature of things. In fact it is difficult to refute Paley's premise that our overwhelming experience of life is of myriad happenings which are shaped to certain ends.

Paley's argument may, indeed, be found more attractive if we take his general principle of intelligibility rather than concentrating upon his analogy of the correlation between a watch and the world. J. S. Mill was quite right to observe that the problem with the watch illustration is that its plausibility rests on the fact that we have *already* encountered watches. Nevertheless, we defend Paley by saying that his contention was that if we have never come across a watch before it would be the principle of design that would impress us. Paley's interest, of course, was not in watches but on a much deeper question: "Does the universe have that quality of design about it?" To which he gave the unequivocal answer, "Yes, in a million different ways – so much so that it dwarfs human ingenuity".

But we are still left with a quandary in spite of Paley's argument. While there is that about the universe which conveys strong suggestions of an intelligent shaping of its parts, we are left with this question: "Is the quality of purpose best explained by the origins of the universe lying in complete chance, however purposive it might now seem to us to be, or really, is it all the product of an Intelligent Source who continues to keep it functioning according to his/its will?"

We shall look at the matter of chance later but for

the time being we simply note the fact that there are those who believe that purpose and design are nothing but the outworking of the world. "Of course the world seems orderly, rational and intelligible. But this is simply because in order to exist at all it must have these characteristics. A personal God does not come into it whatever. Who knows what random, freak chances led to the creation of all things?" This argument reminds me of the saying: "A hen is an egg's way of producing an egg".

This conclusion, however, has received some trenchant criticisms from an unusual source. Fred Hoyle has for many years been no friend to theists and Christian believers. He has always expressed a hearty contempt for views which argue for a divine origin for the universe. However in his book *The Intelligent Universe* he presents a view of the created order which comes very close to that being argued in this book. "Did life start by random processes?", he asks. He answers, "Imagine a blindfolded person trying to solve the Rubik cube. The chance against achieving perfect colour matching is about 50,000,000,000,000,000,000 to 1. These odds are roughly the same as those against just one of our body's 200,000 proteins having evolved randomly, by chance". He argues strongly and cogently against those who assert that life was created spontaneously and therefore accidentally in some primordial soup and he suggests the controversial theory that because life could not have come from blind chance it must have come to earth from "beings" beyond this planet. Whatever we might think about Hoyle's explanation of intelligent life, central to his point is the conviction that there are strong grounds for believing that the universe is intelligent and information-rich and that it is no accident that humanity has an intelligence which is consonant with that of the universe which is our home.

I find myself concluding that the inescapable intimacy that binds mankind and nature together leads to the conclusion that "mind", instead of being an accidental intruder into the realm of matter, is intrinsic to life. The universe, said Sir James Jeans in a celebrated speech, "begins to look more like a great thought than like a great machine". If that is the case, as I believe it to be, we are given an insight into the nature of the Creator who has poured his intelligence as well as his life into the remarkable cosmos which is our home.

So back to Herbie. What would we have made of it if Herbie really was an intelligent, thinking thing? One very possible conclusion is that very likely we would consider this "thing" a person however unusual its appearance or however outside our experience this phenomenon was. Because only "persons" can understand, think or reason and it is only with persons that we can enter into relationships of the deepest kind. At a much deeper level of personhood we judge a person by his or her moral behaviour and capacity to love, honour and respect others. It is in these qualities that Christians find the full flowering of their idea of what it is to be a person. That God is a person they have no doubt because he has shown himself that in Jesus Christ.

5

Has Life any Meaning?

For most of us life conveys a real sense of meaning which we find in the rhythm and joys of life. The majority of our contemporaries live life with a sense of hope although, we have to acknowledge, for most people it is the immediate which concerns them – this year's holiday, family celebrations, or getting a worthwhile job with a decent salary. To lose hope, to lose the sense of worth or meaning, is to lose everything. So then, most of us project a great deal of meaning into our daily lives. All the precious values of human existence keep us going. Without them we could not, and probably would not want to, carry on. That is why we sometimes hear of elderly couples who, when one dies the partner finds himself or herself totally unable to live in any meaningful way again. All real meaning has been taken away from life itself and death together is the only way out. But, equally, that is why many of us take such pleasure and expend so much anxiety on our loved ones because they are for us the meaning of life. We cannot contemplate life without them.

But meaning and value in ordinary life we can accept and understand. Such experiences and relationships make our existence valuable. But is there value and meaning in the universe itself? Can it be that it has been created by a Maker who loves us eternally and who pours meaning into this mysterious creation?

From some points of view the answer might seem to be "no" and the irresistible conclusion is that there is no ultimate or cosmic meaning. We can all think of events which do not fit in with our understanding of a loving God. Take those stories in our newspapers which tell of young children dying of cancer, of accidents which leave children orphans, of tragedies which simply numb us. There does not seem to be any rationale or structure to life which leads ineluctably to the conclusion that we live in a meaningful universe. Of course, this kind of problem is not new. We must not fall into the hubris of thinking that only modern people think such thoughts. The book of Job in the Old Testament is all about this. It appeared that Job found it easy to believe and trust in God when things were going well. Problems began for his belief when everything – including his health – was taken away. We are not now going to take up the issue of pain and evil because that will be considered in the next chapter. The issue which concerns us now is the implication of this; whether there are real grounds for saying that there is meaning and value in life which transcend us and our individual value systems. Again, we must express our concern that our culture has very successfully communicated a moral blight over our society and robbed us of the sense of the transcendent. The separation of "right" and "wrong" from the content of the Christian faith means that morality has lost its ideological basis and few perceive it. The result is that morality has been separated from ideas of God and has been privatised; it has been made largely a matter of personal choice. The corollary of this is serious because if there is no divine basis behind human values all forms of ethical theory are subjective and have as much permanence as a sandcastle.

So it is important to consider whether there are ultimate values in this universe to which we are bound in a permanent relationship of being.

The Christian faith declares firmly that there are, but for the sake of objectivity we must remind ourselves that these cannot be proved in the way that I can prove a mathematical theorem. All we are able to point to are clues that there are values which point beyond us to Someone for whom our behaviour and value systems are important. Nevertheless, I am confident in saying that these are real clues which arch towards the possibility that morality is not a luxury which comes with advanced civilisations – which is somehow dispensable, if we feel inclined – but is anchored in the being and rhythm of the world and as a result is inseparable from mankind's nature to respond to a morality which stands over and against us.

The first and most significant clue is that of morality itself. Moral standards are familiar to us all. Most of us have been shaped by value systems from our childhood. Those of us in the West have been influenced by a Judaeo-Christian morality which embraces both the Ten Commandments and the teaching of Jesus. In other parts of the world other moral codes have given to people a sense of purpose and worth. What is common to all developed moral codes is the common assumption that we are moral and spiritual beings who must respond to claims which transcend them. That is to say, the moral codes together invite us all to grow into a dignity and humanity which is our destiny. But sometimes we wonder whether it is the case that moral codes themselves are nothing more than value systems thrust on people by circumstances, by the conquerors

61

and by convention. Let us consider the issue more carefully. There have been various attempts to explain the
moral element in human nature. Some have held that
the real motive in conduct is self-interest. We do the
things that promote our welfare or happiness, whether
it be as individuals or societies. The classic expression
of this, ironically enough, comes from Satan in the book
of Job where Satan in his discussion with God about the
goodness of Job says with a sneer: "Does Job serve God
for nought?" The implication of the question is that if
all Job's possessions were taken away, the root of his
goodness would soon wither away. According to this
view then, once people find that goodness is no longer
a paying proposition, they will give it up. But the whole
thrust of the book of Job is that integrity of life is more
important than one's life. "Though he slay me, yet will
I trust him", says Job of his God. And what Job wrestles
with, you and I know as well, that while there may
be some whose morality stems from avarice, the only
self-interest that the majority of us recognise in ethical
decisions is the interest of our better self when we know
that a certain course will help others and we say that it
is "right".

Another, and even more popular, theory is that all
morality is nothing more than society's control of its
members. According to this idea our Ideals have their
source in the discovery that certain ways of living and
certain virtues promote the welfare of the tribe and
from these patterns of life society has evolved its norms
in order to safeguard its life and protect the unity of
the family. So, because the habit of theft is bad for
the community, the community forbade it and honesty
became an obligatory moral principle. Because killing

one another destroys the harmony and unity of the community, murder is forbidden. So this theory enthrones the community as the real author of moral values. This looks a very plausible theory and is commonly accepted by many today. Its attraction may reside in the evidence that certain values have clearly been shaped by the needs of the community and changing needs have modified or even rejected what once was thought to be unalterable. Take, for example, the place of women in society. It wasn't all that long ago when western society considered it wrong for women to have the vote or even a profession. Their place was in the home – that was where God had placed them and they should be content with their lot. Few would argue that these days. So it seems that society plays a most significant part in forming our moral codes.

But there are two questions which reveal the weakness of this argument. First, why should it be better for us, in the long run, to be brave rather than cowardly, honest rather than dishonest, pure rather than impure, faithful rather than unfaithful? For such qualities do not always coincide with the benefit of the community. It may well be to the advantage of a tribe to extend its boundaries by pillaging, rape and widespread destruction. It may seem, then, that such actions are acceptable because they advance the good of the tribe. I have not met anybody who would argue this. In point of fact, such qualities of honesty, goodness and bravery – to name but a few – do work out for the wellbeing of the community in spite of the experience that they do not always work out for the material benefit of those who live such generous lives. At the international level we are discovering today that goodwill, humanity, freedom, forgiveness and tolerance are among the values which advance civilisation and that national selfishness and moral anarchy are threatening the very being of human existence. There can be only one explanation for the existence of such "soft" altruistic standards and that is that life is meant to be lived in this way – that such laws of conduct are not imposed on us through the needs of the community but rather they emerge from the constitution of our being.

The second question is this: Is it not the case that moral codes have arisen from charismatic leaders and from minority groups rather than from society as a whole? It is an undeniable fact that in nearly every case when a great moral teacher has appeared, society has at first rejected him because his message has condemned the practices and values of society. We note, for example, that so many pioneers of reform have had to go to the stake for their beliefs or have had to struggle for recognition. If society originated the moral laws why was it that when the prophets of the Old Testament and the greatest of all moral teachers, Jesus Christ, appeared, society rejected their teaching and authority?

It seems very clear then that the sense of moral obligation has deeper roots than our own social advantage. It is not in fact the case that our own good is the reason why "goodness" has authority over us. Rather, we seek the good because it is right and not because it is to our advantage. It is only when we are prepared to listen to the voice of conscience and follow it that our true humanity and calling is discovered. André Gide – an immoral libertine with a nagging conscience – spoke more perceptively than he realised when he wrote: "Je ne suis qu'un petit garcon qui s'amuse, double de pasteur protestant qui l'ennuie" (I am just a little boy having fun, with a protestant minister nagging away inside me). That is to say, he was aware, however dimly, of obligations which challenged his instincts and desires.

So the conditional and relativising attitude which dismisses all morality as stemming from the needs of society must be rejected as inadequate. Most of us do not view ethical responses in that way anyway. We regard morality as having an over-arching and eternal significance. Morality is true regardless of time and place. Murder, we assume, would always be wrong whether one is a Caligula living in the first century or Hitler living in the twentieth century. Standards of goodness, decency, honour, integrity or honesty (among other great virtues which make a civilisation great) are true whatever the time and place. We do find ourselves therefore postulating "absolute" standards of right and wrong. This was at the heart of the famous debate between Bertrand Russell and the Roman Catholic philosopher, Thomas Coplestone. Russell had declared that there were no absolute values as such; all we could say was that there exist values which we deem important. To this Coplestone cited the then recent Nuremburg trials in which Nazi criminals had been convicted of crimes against humanity. If there are no absolutes, he asked, it is not immediately obvious what was the conceptual basis for the trials. Crimes against humanity suggest that there exists a moral standard that all are agreed the Nazis contravened. Many of those accused could cite that they were carrying out the edicts of the State or following the orders of superiors. Yet the Trial expressed the unanimous verdict of the nations that those condemned had broken a moral law which was absolute and eternal. There can be little doubt that Coplestone had the better of that argument because when we are faced with issues of such magnitude we are convinced of the reality of moral facts which call us to a higher standard of humanity than that of our present experience.

It is true that we do not need the hypothesis God for such a morality. I want to make it very clear that even in a godless universe most of us would still expect cruelty to be wrong and evil. We all know people who do not have a "faith" to speak of but who live honourable and good lives. Nevertheless in a godless universe the concepts of "wrongdoing" and "goodness" are going to have completely different meanings from that of a morality anchored in belief in God. For example, I may say as a non-believer: "Although I do not believe in God I still firmly believe that it is right to be honest and a person of integrity. For me moral standards are vital for society, my personal life and the community that I belong to." It is obvious however that the basis of my ethics will depend for its validity not upon a God who gives to such values eternal significance, but upon our inbuilt feelings that certain things are wrong and others are right.

Secondly, while it would be the honourable thing to be good and righteous in a godless universe, it does not seem to be the most logical way of performing. If this life is all, then choosing an ethic which means putting other people first seems an astonishingly illogical way to live. As Professor Oliver O'Donovan puts it: "No earthly good can be worth dying for unless there is a heavenly good that is worth living for". This observation goes to the heart of the malaise of western civilisation. The loss of the transcendent in our society has led to the questioning of "ultimate sacrifice". Whereas our forebears could face death with equanimity and consider it worthwhile to lay down one's life for another because of the greater hope and destiny to which one was called, this consoling synthesis is no longer at the centre of our concept of life. In a world where values are relative and transitory too great a demand then is placed upon other appeals to make them truly convincing. A recent example is the Falklands War which led to the loss of hundreds of lives on both sides. What was the war about? The question of the sovereignty of a small island? A matter of honour? We could well question whether either or both of these things are worth the death of one young soldier let alone thousands. We might well wonder about the reaction now of bereaved wives and families to that war. It is doubtful whether they see it as a necessary conflict which justified the deaths of those who went to war. We wonder if in ten years' time a deal is struck in which sovereignty passes to the Argentine by gradual stages, would not that very act negate the eternal sacrifices made? The point I am making is the very futility of acts of that nature *if* the values we are living by and dying for are not in some sense eternal and relate to God who gives to life its rationality and meaning. Otherwise such acts are basically tragic and meaningless.

This last conclusion, of course, has been reached by serious philosophers in recent years. Friedrich Nietzsche argued that in the absence of God everything is permitted. This view has been taken up by existential writers like Jean-Paul Sartre for whom the absence of God was not only a terrifying nightmare but also, curiously, a liberating experience; because now man has only himself to rely upon and this, Sartre thought, would lead to humanity's growth. But "good" without God makes moral values relative and subordinate to what is "good" for us. It will be seen that this line of argument may lead into a sharp individualism [what is good for "me"] and it may equally have a nihilistic edge to it [if we are all doomed to annihilation and meaning does not exist, so what the hell].

I have already agreed, however, that even if God did not exist there would be reason to be moral beings. I am not advocating that if this universe is a random happening that we should all behave like animals. Of course not. We would all affirm that human life, our love for others and our respect for their views would demand from each one of us a morality that was in accord with the well-ordering of society. The "golden rule" of Jesus – "Do unto others what they would do to you" – applies equally to an atheistic culture as to one founded on Christian insights. But I would like to go on to suggest that although I do not need God to be a moral person, at the very least the existence of God gives to morality a depth, coherence and rational framework that is otherwise lacking. You see, within the Christian tradition we can easily explain why non-religious people are moral people – it is because they too are made in the image of God and bear the stamp of his likeness. It is an element of our theology that to be a human being at all is to be aware of moral strivings, feelings of guilt and sin, and feelings of freedom and slavery. At the heart of this understanding of humanity is the teaching that humanity has gone fundamentally astray, that we are unable to find the true God unaided because we are fallen and sinful. This is the famous doctrine of *original sin* which, simply stated, means that there is a fundamental flaw in our human nature which stops us becoming the kind of people we would like to be. G. K.

Chesterton once said perceptively that of all Christian doctrines original sin was the only directly provable one because the evidence was all too obvious.

But why should "God" give to morality a more rational framework than, say, the argument that morality is but the outworking of conventions in society, or our corporate experience that certain behaviour is more satisfactory for us all? I have already answered this to some extent in my observations above concerning the fact that for the Christian, God is himself the justification for the way we behave. If I decide, in a country violently opposed to the Christian faith, that I must act in such a way that I could incur the wrath of the State and face the death penalty, I do so because I have a system of transcendental values which is true whatever may happen to me. In a similar way, martyrs for just causes are clearly protesting for values which are not transitory and relative but for things which concern them so deeply that they can only act in that way. So, for example, the political and religious dissidents in Soviet Russia willingly endure separation, physical pain, mockery and in some cases death because they reject as basically inhuman (and Godless) a system which allows no other point of view but its own. However, I think we can say a little more than that. It is accepted by many of us that the reality of morality is written in large letters in the actual experience and history of mankind. And it is an agreed assumption, I find, that there are moral facts, absolute areas of "right" and "wrong", which stand over us judging us by standards we all recognize and calling us to a personhood which, as yet, eludes most of us. And I find a tacit acknowledgement by most people that such laws are valid for all people and all time.

We are not, of course, talking about values which may depend upon cultural ways of behaviour; matters concerning the smooth running of society and aspects of convention. Rather, our concern is upon the fact of moral worth which transcends culture. For example, we take it for granted that killing another person in cold blood will be as wrong in AD 2500 as it is now. And, for that matter, we cannot conceive of a society in which stealing, lying, cruelty etc. could ever be considered socially acceptable acts. Not only would they undermine society and eventually destroy it but we actually do believe that they are wrong, per se. But the nub of the problem is this. While most of us actually *believe* that such acts are wrong no convincing argument can be adduced to *prove* this fact. Morality cannot prove God but what it can do is point to him and the values which are at his heart. Such values will be the dignity of humanity, our intrinsic worth, our moral nature and our ability to respond to claims of "oughtness" and "rightness", our ability to grow in selfless action and love for others and our capacity for self-sacrifice which, on the face of it, seems madness. All this, and much more, points beyond ourselves and cries for explanation. Does all this simply come from ourselves or are these elements of a bonding with the divine which has all the dimensions of an Imperative which cannot be denied or ignored?

Another area which must be examined briefly are those qualities of human existence, art, beauty and pleasure, which also point beyond ourselves to the possibility of another origin. Just before Christmas in 1986 my wife and I enjoyed a brief holiday near Hereford. As I had never visited the Cathedral before I decided to spend the Saturday afternoon in it. I pushed open the Cathedral doors and was hit by an explosion of sound that filled the place and my soul as well. What I discovered was that in the Cathedral a visiting orchestra and local choir were rehearsing Dvorak's *Te Deum* for an evening concert. The richness of the sound and the beauty of the music was so bewitchingly wonderful that all the listeners on that grey afternoon were taken up into a world so different from the one we were inhabiting. This experience brought home to me the way that music and poetry stand out as marvellous vehicles for the language of the soul. And yet, they need not be seen in that way. The instruments, after all, are only things made by people and the performers are obviously only mortal. Even the music, when reduced to squiggles on paper, does not appear to be any more than the cold symbols of human beings trying to entertain. But that reductionism is dismissed immediately by most of us because we know how music and art in their varying forms can enlarge the human spirit and take us to levels of perception and emotional heights that nothing else can do. Little wonder that such areas of life have been harnessed by religion over the centuries and encouraged by mainstream faiths because of the very evocative force they release.

If this is so, two very important corollaries follow. The first is a challenge to language in our culture. Perhaps the barrenness of spirit today is related to the debasing of language as a mere counter of knowledge. That is to say, our tendency to limit words to conveying reality as if they were merely a way through to knowledge. But the world of imagination forces us to ask: Are we not depriving ourselves of a world of colour and richness by making the plain meaning primary and the metaphor and poetry of language secondary? Could it not be true that the world of literature in all its forms together with the long history of creative art are not external to knowledge and the meaning of life but essential components within it, possessing power to comprehend spiritual realities in life? The writer and poet Coleridge was intensely aware of the link between art and faith, between knowledge and religion. He remarked: "When I worship let me unify . . . to be wise I must". Or as the theologian Schleiermacher once observed, "What the word makes clear, music must make alive".

The second observation takes us to the heart of another dichotomy in modern life, namely our tendency to separate faith and life. For the Christian the two are inseparably connected. To be a Christian and to be a human being are essentially one. But for the non-believer, Christianity and indeed all faiths are culturally by-products of civilisations invented to meet human needs and aspirations. They, together with art and any form of knowledge, are aspects of the flowering of human development but have no intrinsic value over and above that.

Yet, the evidence in fact points in the opposite direction. Faith in God is not a cultural accretion but an essential part of culture. Toynbee said long ago: "The great civilisations of the world do not produce the great religions as a kind of cultural by-product; in a real sense the great religions are the foundations on which the great civilisations rest". As far as Christianity is concerned, for more than a millenium it has supplied the meaning and aim of individual and corporate existences. It has fed the living stream of western culture in such a rich way that our civilisation is incomprehensible without it. Yet for the last hundred and fifty years this heritage of faith has been deliberately jettisoned in order to show that science alone – or some other pathway – can provide humanity with a better framework for life. Here is another element in the "God Robbery" we are exploring because culture devoid of the faith that gave it birth is but a new name for a new paganism. Chip away at the cement of faith and the foundations of humanity will be seen to be very unstable indeed; strip away firm belief in God and eventually we will start disbelieving in ourselves and everything we hold dear. Well did T. S. Eliot write: "Man is man because he can realise spiritual realities not because he can invent them".

Good, Evil and God

Two years ago my mother died. She was 76 years of age and she had lived a full and happy life. But her last year had been an absolute hell. Cancer of the tongue had developed which required radiotherapy. In spite of modern drugs she was in constant pain and, with distress, we her children watched with sadness her losing battle against the disease. Towards the end she went downhill rapidly. I happened to be with her holding her hand when she died. As I looked at her face, wasted away with pain and hardly recognizable as my dear mother, I wondered where God was in this situation. I found myself asking bitterly: "God – here is a Christian lady who has served you faithfully down the years. Now look at the pain and discomfort she has had to bear. Is this how you treat your friends?" Of course, I acknowledge that it was grief speaking at that moment. My mother would have been the first to have reminded me firmly that God's love transcends all evil and all human suffering. Nevertheless, in reacting as I did, I was echoing the experience of millions of people who feel in pain and suffering the absence of God.

Very few of us doubt that the problem of evil is the single greatest obstacle to faith. The case for God would be simply overwhelming if this issue did not separate intelligent people from the concept of a loving God. We respect those for whom evil forbids faith. However, sadly, yet increasingly, I find people today accepting an attitude that says tacitly there is no personal God behind the things that are, but rather blind, unreasoning fate. "We can't understand it", apparently goes the attitude "but whatever will be, will be". Such a stance is not founded upon careful thought and study but drawn from a culture which has already come to the conclusion that life is purposeless. Again we have in this matter another example of the way modern people are being conned into adopting an attitude which is simply borrowed from the prevailing, hostile spiritual environment of our time. We need to ask then: Is it a fact that the problem of evil is so overwhelming that it cancels out all arguments for God's presence in the world? We must look at the issues involved.

The problem of evil can be put into two different categories. First there is the moral evil caused by man's evil to man. We can think of happenings which create further evil, such as war leading to famine or concentration camps resulting in the suffering of innocent children. In this category we could put the simply awful suffering of the Jewish people in the last war to which we have already referred. The estimate of eight million human beings dying, many in the most appalling and degrading ways, will always be an indictment on twentieth-century civilisation. At Auschwitz there died completely the concept of man's perfectibility. Until that time there were many people who believed that through self improvement – education, medical care, etc. – human beings would grow into a god-like state of well-being and grace. There is, it was thought, no limit upon the achievements humankind is capable of. Many believed there was no limit to humankind's destiny. Auschwitz revealed the folly of such grand hopes. But for many committed

Jews the nightmare raised the most serious doubts about God's activity with his so-called people. The Jewish writer Milac Makovec explained that his rejection of God stems from the evil in the world: "I cannot combine faith in God with Auschwitz". As mentioned earlier the Jewish writer, Professor Richard Rubenstein put it more trenchantly: "How can Jews believe in an omnipotent, beneficent God after Auschwitz?" Rubenstein's answer led him to conclude that although there is a "God" of some description we are bereft of him. We stand alone in a cold, silent, unfeeling cosmos, unaided by any purposeful power beyond our own resources. He appeals to his fellow Jews to revise their theology and to reinterpret their faith which has to find a new form and focus in the preservation of the religious community.

The Jewish experience is not everybody's experience, however. And, we should add, not all Jews are convinced that a radical revisionism is necessary. Yet it crystallizes the central issue as far as man-centred moral evil is concerned. *Why* could not have God intervened? It does not seem beyond God's power – if, that is, he is all powerful – to intervene in the mess that we make of his creation. We can think of hundreds of examples of the problem and we are left with our questions.

The second category of moral evil is the evil endemic in creation and life. We need only think of little children born with defects which range from a harelip to Down's Syndrome or cancer. We think of tragedies which strike regardless of values of right and wrong. The good are as likely to suffer as the bad in the lottery of life. As often is the case, the case is put in its sharpest form in literature which explores the nature of the world. In Dostoyevsky's *The Brothers Karamazov*, Ivan protests vehemently against a world in which innocent human beings, including innocent children, suffer hideous cruelties at the hands of those who have power over them. Ivan cannot understand how such a world can be the creation of a good God or how a just creator can permit such suffering and fail to use his power on behalf of the victims. The extent of suffering, Ivan believes, points to indifference at the heart of the universe. He is led to renounce Christianity's claims for a good God, courteously refusing a ticket to a heaven which is based on such suffering, by saying, "I renounce the higher harmony altogether. It is not worth the tears of that one tortured child . . ." Yet, we must understand, this passionate expression of atheism comes from an artist who writes from THE SIDE OF THE CHRISTIAN FAITH. Dostoyevsky does not reject the Christian faith; but he does point at the real world and the real questions that challenge faith.

A similar point is made by Albert Camus in his book *The Plague* although now from a different point of view. Camus did not share Dostoyevsky's faith but he did share his concern for a world which did not appear to express moral values. Dr Rieux, one of the central characters in the book, betrays the same angry reaction following the agonizing death of a child. The priest observes that the death is only revolting because we do not understand it and says that: "Perhaps we should love what we cannot understand". The doctor replies angrily, "No, Father! I have a different idea of love. Until my dying day I shall refuse to love a scheme of things in which children are put to torture." We can agree emphatically that Dr Rieux's response is more "Christian" than that of the Priest's, whose superficial attitude seems indifferent and callous.

Yet Camus is painfully aware that in rejecting the possibility of God, such concepts as justice, morality, honour and kindness have to be redefined. "Can one be a saint without God?" asks Tarrou in the same book. The question is never answered even though the book struggles to find the value of human existence in a creation without a Creator.

While it is important to feel the awfulness of evil we must start our discussion of it in the context of good. The fact of the matter is that we do not live in a universe of unmitigated evil. To read some books you would think so. If the cosmos is as blind, irrational and indifferent as some people claim, truth, beauty, love, meaning, goodness, purity, honesty and other values become problems themselves and require explanation. It is a fact, as we observed earlier, that for the majority of us life can have great purpose. Evil – seen, that is, from the viewpoint of most of us – is more like an element which breaks into good rather than good interrupting a scheme of things in which evil is the normal currency. The latter is clearly not the case. This planet, for example, is congenial for our wellbeing and survival. Mankind has flourished and multiplied over the centuries and within our environment there has been a sufficiency of raw products to take us from the cave to the space shuttle. Our supremacy over our habitat may not be enough to lead inexorably to the thought of there being of necessity a personal Maker (although Christians believe that this would not be an illogical deduction) but it is consonant with the world as being good, when we take all the elements together.

If that is the case, then, we have to account for the evil in the world and try to explain why God does not intervene when things go wrong. There are at

least four possible responses to this issue. We shall leave
unconsidered such answers as "evil is only imaginary" or
"evil is God's judgement on sinners". The first is clearly
and demonstrably wrong and the second, whilst obviously more plausible and true as a general truth, does
not fit the nature of the evidence because the innocent
are involved in suffering. If suffering is the result of
personal sin it can't be theirs and, indeed, the theory
would make God a monster.

One possible answer is that pain and evil are inevitable
consequences of the world being as it is. Swinburne,
a modern philosopher, argues that if God wanted to
create an environment for humanity's relationship with
himself, and his moral and spiritual growth, it has to be
a world similar to our own in which wasted suffering and
natural evil are present. According to this view, moral
and spiritual responses come through the challenges of
life. It assumes that in a static universe where there is
no conflict, no opposition between good and evil, no
disasters and no errors of any kind, mankind would be
morally static and moribund.

There is enough truth in this theory to impress. It
is agreed that change, trouble and disorder are elements
that spur growth. Certainly our experience of life shows
that adversity makes people grow morally and spiritually
and draws forth outstanding acts of behaviour. There
would be no acts of mercy if people were in no danger,
no acts of heroism if others did not require saving, no
goodness if all were good, and so we could go on. But
the argument leaves me unconvinced. I want to ask, how
do we know that a perfect world could not produce moral
acts such as the ones listed? Why is it necessary to assume
that a paradise on earth would be morally static? And,

for that matter, speaking on behalf of the half-believer or non-believer, we wonder about the long ages of history where natural calamities occurred before mankind's arrival which had nothing to do with our moral growth. Indeed, this argument suggests that heaven is morally static so that it appears that growth is impossible. Surely this goes against the Christian conviction that life in God has endless, exciting possibilities for growth and development. I for one do not believe in a heaven which is morally stagnant and I am equally sure we don't need battles and adversity to make this possible!

A second theory argues that free will requires a world which is not self-limited in any form. According to this argument God's ultimate purpose in creating for himself human persons, made for his glory and made in his image, entails the creation of a world in which freedom is at its heart. In such a world God necessarily limits himself and takes a risk in allowing humankind to have such freedom that human sinfulness is allowed full scope and evil may run riot. Freedom and free will must, according to this argument, be real gifts of God and part of the constituent make-up of life, otherwise we will end up with a crazy world in which God keeps leaping in and out to intervene when his favourites get into trouble. Such a world and a God would be ludicrous. Freedom and free will will result in mistakes, error and growth. Such a theory is not without its attractions. We know that much evil is directly attributable to man's cruelty and evil. The holocaust is a sad example of this fact. It cannot be the case, we may think, that God must be blamed for something which has to be laid at humanity's door.

But, again, there are aspects to this which trouble me.

Does free will demand a world in which God apparently abandons the world to the devices of evil? If free will is directly attributable to God's created act of giving us freedom, it seems beyond the power of God for him to be able to create a universe in which free will is exercised in a world in which goodness is not overthrown. The point must be pressed home; we might well ask, "What is God doing when suffering and evil out of all proportion are afflicted by evil people on the innocent?" And this is at the heart of the matter – we are not talking about suffering in reasonable proportions to the situation but gross, shocking evils which defy description. This is the point that some radical Jewish theologians make about the holocaust. The awfulness of the situation raised the most serious doubts concerning their central understanding of God. Brought up on the belief that he is the faithful God of Israel his absence when his people went through their agony was a question that had to be answered. So, while it is possible to understand that God restrains his power because he has given free will to his creatures, the APPARENT abnegation of his power resulting in the experience of absence of God and the triumph of evil cries out for an answer. Indeed, do we not find at this point the cry of the cross: "My God, why have you forsaken me?"

A third theory associated with Bernard Lonergan, perhaps the greatest Roman Catholic philosopher of this century, questions the use of the phrase, "problem of evil". What do we mean when we call evil a "problem", he asks. He points out that we commonly judge God's purposes in the world by whether or not a thing occurs which is good or bad for us. A friend is tragically killed, someone known to us is struck down by a rare disease, a child dies. Because such things happen which do not accord with our understanding of how God ought to act we conclude that the universe is inexplicable and "evil" is a negation of good. But, argues Lonergan, we cannot assess the matter in such personal terms. Our criterion is irrationality when, in fact, the world is intensely rational. Things occur because there are reasons for them doing so. Earthquakes happen for physical reasons; the avalanche falls because of factors which can be understood scientifically; the disease is attributable to causes which can be known. So, if one lives in California or in Bangladesh, we must not complain too bitterly when the earthquake or the flood occurs – because we know that these places are susceptible to such physical "evils". We call the problem "evil" because we judge the order of the world by whether or not it works to our wellbeing.

There is an awesome logic about Lonergan's approach and I happen to think that he is close to the truth of the matter. But a few problems remain, particularly with regard to the nature of God. Even if he has removed the element of the problem of evil, he has created a further one about God himself. What is Lonergan's God like who allows such things to happen? What are his purposes in allowing that little child to die before her time? We can allow the irresistible logic which demands that leukaemia may issue in death if unhealed but it is happening to a child made, according to Christian faith, in the image of God and it is God who directly or indirectly is the cause of the problem.

However I do find Lonergan's theory helpful and suggest that its insights should be held in tension with our fourth theory which takes up the theme of PURPOSE. We know that one of the reasons we can accept the death of an old man, whilst bitterly deploring the death of a young mother, has something to do with the unfulfilled nature of human destiny. We can say of the first, "He has had a fine innings. Sad to see him go, though. We shall miss him but he was failing towards the end." But of the latter death we are inclined to say, "How very sad. What a loss to us all. What a happy person she was. And the children are going to miss her awfully."

Our attitude to both situations is linked with our understanding of fulfilment. "Good" and "evil" are anchored in our estimate of a worthwhile life. What has happened has not lived up to our natural expectation. It is not fair that the young woman should be taken at that time. We rebel against the injustice of it. But what we are failing to observe in drawing these conclusions is that the issue is not merely about evil but evil in the context of good. We are implicitly granting that the badness occurs in the setting of success – of good being present. We are passionately aware of the presence of justice, good, human dignity and other values and there is a diminution of such qualities, we feel, in this or that particular case. So, for example, that sick child is a child who is sick. That is to say, she is a human person who at this point is being held back from her destiny to be a whole and healthy girl. In Christian theology this idea is sometimes called "privation". That is, the person is affected by something which deprives her, either temporarily or permanently, of the possibility of growing to her full potential. Thus, to say that a loaf of bread is "bad" is not to say that it is not a loaf of bread but that it fails to come up to our expectations. Seen, then, from this perspective the presence of evils in the world are elements which deprive us of what we assume to be our rightful heritage as human beings.

Two observations may be made of this theory immediately. First, it takes seriously the fact of evil but it does not directly attribute it to God. Evil is the non-obtaining of good. It is the falling short of the perfection which is its true destiny and is an incompleteness which is not God's will.

Second, the Christian faith does not consider evil in any way final or decisive. However awful it may be, and however its tragic dimensions may affect every aspect of human life, evil cannot cut God's people off from their destiny in him. In other words evil will not have the last word; God's purposes will triumph over the short-lived evils brought upon human beings by a world in which the human drama is set. As some theologians put it we need to see this world from the viewpoint of *sub specie aeternatis*, from God's ultimate purpose for his creation; failure to take this into our reckoning will result in a one-dimensional view of human existence which is the bankrupt legacy of twentieth-century thought. Let us take, for example, an analogy from a tadpole pool. Let us allow that within the pool relationships there is constituted the heart of morality. Good and evil are seen in terms of their welfare. So, if a thing happens that makes them happy, wealthy or "fulfilled", that is "good". If something happens which seems to deny their destiny we call that happening "bad". But, still playing with our analogy, we allow that the true destiny of the tadpoles is not to live and die as tadpoles but to grow up to become frogs, then what we tacitly assumed to be "good" (from within the pond) for the tadpoles is now seen not to be so when viewed from a different perspective. Similarly, if this life is all, we might well judge goodness and its opposite from such criteria as the length of life, standard of living, peace and prosperity, the happiness of our children, and so on. But if our destiny finds its true fulfilment in an eternal fellowship with God which is begun in this life and flowers not only in a fulfilled life now (for many of us) but also into a glorious life beyond death, then we begin to see that God may have a different understanding of the meaning of human existence and the place of struggle, tragedy, defeat, and weakness in its constitution.

We have glanced at four possible approaches to the problem of evil. We have made no attempt to minimise the revulsion we all feel in the presence of this ugly blasphemy which distorts not only human life but the whole of creation. Nevertheless we have also seen that when we remove it from its context in goodness or exaggerate its prominence we do not do justice to a world which carries the marks of a good creator. Evil is the blackness in the tapestry of life but there are many other colours there and, as one of the theories mentioned above observed, we need the blackness in order for the other colours to be seen in all their splendour. That may well be the case. However, I will not pretend that the problem of evil has been solved or that the theist can easily avoid the difficult task of explaining its presence in a world which we claim to be the creation of a loving Heavenly Father.

There is a final point that we must observe if we really wish to have a rounded view of the whole matter. The Christian world-view does not include a God out there who watches helplessly, yet with compassion, as his people suffer. We believe firmly in wholehearted, committed suffering love. Christian faith is summed up in the good news that the cross is the gateway of life with God and there we see God identifying with sin and suffering. To leave the cross out is to miss something important about the character of God and the nature of his love.

It may seem that the problem is essentially unresolvable. In one sense we have to admit it is. Reason cannot take us all the way into believing in a God who created the world and gives us its meaning. We acknowledge that we all bring to such a question our own presuppositions and prejudices. I am a Christian and it is impossible for me to consider the issue from the standpoint of unbelief. I cannot suspend either my critical faculties or my faith. And neither can an agnostic reading these words. He too approaches the issue with his own set of prejudices and presuppositions. It may seem then that such fixed positions cancel each other out and we have to be content with a resigned agnosticism. But the Christian will want to answer that faith cannot be built on reason or objective facts alone; it also comes from the experience of Christians who claim that they have met the living God. In Christ they have found him, not as an indifferent, cold deity who leaves them to get on with the task of living, but as a father who cares and loves. To the question of "experience" we must now turn.

What has Experience to say about God?

So far in this book our exploration into God has been limited to rational argument. We have been trying to show that belief in God is "reasonable" and can be accepted by modern western people. Now I happen to believe that this is the case and I am not alone in holding this conviction with confidence. For literally millions of people, only acceptance of a God who creates and cares makes sense of this world. But such an acceptance falls far short of the Christian God who confronts men and women not as a mysterious deity but as the "living God", the creator God who is as a being to be worshipped and adored. I, personally, cannot work up much enthusiasm for a First Cause or a "merely probable God" who is just the abstraction of human minds. Such a belief would be too dreary for words and would not propel faith in the way that a real encounter with the Living God would.

This powerful confrontation has been viewed in many different ways but all these forms focus in what we call "experience". People claim that they have "found" God, "met" God, felt his "touch" of power, peace, comfort or challenge, and experienced his "love". This should not be too surprising, of course. If there is a personal God, as Alec Vidler used to say, it is in our personal experience that we should expect to find the strongest evidence of his existence. Indeed, experiences claimed to be of God and of messages from him are so widespread, not only in time but also throughout the world, that they must be examined to see if here there are intimations of the presence of God. The problem, however, is that of evaluating the myriad forms that the experience of God takes and assessing the reality or falsehood of such claims. Are they, we have to ask, proofs of God as such? Certainly they seem to be so for the person who claims to have met God but what about those of us who stand by sceptically and listen?

Now in the majority of cases we cannot deny the sincerity of those who say that they have met God. But how do we know that it is God that they have met? After all, if my house is burgled and I catch a glimpse of the burglar fleeing from the house and say to the police, "Jack Brown is the culprit", the reasonable deduction is that I have met Mr Brown before, otherwise I could not have known his name. So when a person says, "Last week I met God", or "I had a wonderful experience of his love", we could reasonably deduce that God was already a familiar concept to her, otherwise the claim would not have been put in that form. The suspicion then is that some degree of pre-conditioning has gone on to make the idea of God a reality before the experience takes place. It is a fact, for example, that the phenomena of appearances of the Blessed Virgin Mary which occur almost exclusively in Roman Catholic countries strongly suggest to the outsider that such visions have been influenced by popular Catholic expectation that when God appears directly to people he is going to take a Marian shape. I am not for one minute questioning the reality of such experiences but the facts compel us to note the way the background of belief shapes the nature of the experience. Of course it is arguably the case, we must admit, that no one can come to an experience without some idea of what is being experienced and what the experience does is to "fill out" the nature of the teaching already received. For example, when St Paul had his life-shattering Damascus road experience it was unexpected, confusing and yet consonant with all that had preceded it. On the one hand it was an experience which destroyed his previous beliefs about Jesus Christ and his followers. Yet on the other hand we can perhaps surmise that it was in line with his deep-seated thoughts about the strange man from Nazareth and thus led to a devastating rearrangement of his theology. It was therefore not totally surprising.

But we need to be sure that religious experience is in fact the experience of meeting an objective God and not simply that of wish fulfilment. The idea that "if you believe a thing hard enough, it will happen" is not unknown in history. Honesty compels us to acknowledge that we have no real objective way of knowing. We have to realise that other people's experiences are totally inaccessible to us as, indeed, are all the really deep intimate moments of life when they occur to others. If someone says to me, "I am in love with this adorable girl!", I have to accept his word that there is a reality to his awed words, flushed expression and wide eyes. That it could be put down to indigestion is a possibility – but I would be a cynic to suspect this has to be the case at first appearance, unless, indeed, I know he suffers from indigestion!

A few months ago I led a conference in New Zealand and spoke to a lady in her fifties, a well educated and thoughtful woman who sadly was in perpetual pain with a degenerative spinal problem and who had problems of depression. I met her again a few weeks later and she was clearly a different person. She told me that she was healed. Her back was normal – according to her doctor – and her mental attitude was obviously better. She was so much better that I even doubted at first if this was the woman I had talked and prayed with earlier. Her claim was that, through my prayers and through a healing conference she attended, she was now wholly better through the direct intervention of the Holy Spirit. She was now whole. I was overjoyed to see this but I must admit that at the time my innate scepticism within clashed with my real conviction that God can and does heal today. But when he does we are astounded and dumbfounded – even those of us who should not be! We get somehow nervous when we stumble on the frightening fact – as it surely is – that God is personally at work in the world today. But how could I be sure that what she was claiming was the truth? Further investigation confirmed the woman's story; she was infinitely better and her friends vouched for the startling return to full health in body and mind. However, what I had no access to was to the actual experience which led to that healing. To return to my question, "How could I be sure that it was an experience of God?" Yes, I could have jumped to the conclusion that the experience of healing was due to wish fulfilment but I find that explanation, in this lady's case, far more unconvincing than that God's power was directly at work within her restoring her to full health.

It then seems to be the case that there are no tests to check on such claims if, that is, the claims of others can not be verified for certain. However, while it may well be the case that there are no objective scientific tests we can apply, there are, as we shall see, some observations that will assist us in discerning whether the claim is true or false. But before we consider that, we must outline the main types of religious experience and note what they have meant to the individuals concerned.

Within the Christian tradition the experience of God has taken many different forms. Down the centuries people have claimed to have met God in a variety of ways which, for them, have been unique and life changing. We can, however, distinguish five main forms.

First of all, one type focusses on "sight" whether or not the experience has been physical or spiritual. Some have claimed to have actually "seen" God. This type of experience is frequent in scripture; we think of Abraham and the angelic beings who meet and talk with him; we think of St Paul and his vision of God which resulted in blindness and eventual restoration of sight. But this experience is not confined to the covers of sacred history. It has also been claimed by many down the centuries and in our own day. For example, the appearances of the Virgin Mary claimed to have been seen by many at the Yugoslavian town of Medjugorje belong to this type. It is difficult for those of us who have never had a visual encounter with spiritual reality to know how to react to such claims. For the moment we must suspend judgement and listen to the stories that people tell of their meeting with the numinous.

Then, second, there is another type of experience which, whilst less direct, is no less vivid and meaningful to the recipient. This is where people have encountered the presence of God through dreams and sensory experiences which have led to accounts of being "overwhelmed" or "enveloped" by God. Dr F. C. Happold describes in his book *Religious Faith and Twentieth Century Man* the story of his own experience: "It happened in my room in Peterhouse in the evening of 1 February 1913, when I was an undergraduate at Cambridge. If I say Christ came to me I should be using conventional words which would carry no precise meaning; for Christ comes to men and women in different ways. When I tried to record the experience at the time I used the imagery of the Holy Grail; it seemed to me to be just like that. There was, however, no sensible vision. There was just the room, with its shabby furniture and the red shaded lamp on the table. But the room was filled with a Presence, which in a strange way was both about me and within me, like light or warmth. I was overwhelmingly possessed by Someone who was not myself, and yet I felt I was more myself than I had ever been before. I was filled with an intense happiness, an almost unbearable joy, such as I had never known before and never known since. And over all was a deep sense of peace and security and certainty. Some experiences of this sort, which I have found recorded, lasted a very short time. Mine lasted several hours . . ." The actress Sarah Miles also stated in a Press interview that she had been converted from atheism by mystical experiences of this sort which overwhelmed her for no apparent reason.

We note that the "reality" of the two types of experiences we have just considered is conveyed through sensory perception. Happold, for example, resists the idea that it was a direct visual encounter in his room but he is equally sure that the entire meeting was real and, we might say, sacramental. This raises the question about the relationship between material and spiritual realities. Somehow what people are struggling to convey is the way the ordinary is transfused as well as transformed by the divine presence. Remarkably, St Augustine, that great philosopher and possibly the first great psychologist, described his conversion in ways which recall the five senses; he heard, saw, smelled, tasted and touched God – or was it not all along the case that God took the initiative and encountered him? So he wrote, "You called to me, you cried aloud to me, you broke my barrier of deafness. You shone upon me, your radiancy enveloped me. You put my blindness to flight. You shed your fragrance about me. I drew breath and I gasp for your sweet odour. I tasted you and I hunger and thirst for you. You touched me and I am inflamed with love of your peace."

Third, there are experiences which many Christians have had where the experience of meeting God has resulted in a state of peace, wellbeing or calm awareness of God's presence. Here are two illustrations taken from different traditions: "I was kneeling one evening in the quietness of the chapel before the Blessed sacrament as my habit was", wrote a Roman Catholic lady, "when a deep and contented peace came upon me. I had the strange sensation that I was not alone; that someone was with me. An indescribable feeling of joy and happiness welled up within me. I was so glad – my heart seemed to be bursting with delight at his presence. When I left the chapel after what seemed such a brief and wonderful time I discovered I had been there for two and a half hours!" From a different tradition within the Church a young man narrates his experience in the following way: "I was in my second year at Oxford University and had been going to church for a few months. I was not much of a church-goer, to be honest, but one evening I went to a

Guest Service and listened to a lively sermon which made me aware of the claims of Christ on my life. I went back to my lodgings convinced of the reality of the Christian faith. The preacher had spoken about asking Jesus into your life. Not quite sure what this meant I sat on my bed and thought about it and realized that I wanted to be a full-blooded Christian. So in the quietness of my room I prayed that God would accept me, and I can't claim that I heard a voice or anything like that. I just felt that I wasn't talking to the ceiling but that I was accepted. Christianity was now real for me."

Into the category of the experience of God's presence we can put John Wesley's conversion when he felt "my heart was strangely warmed". Surely that must be the understatement of all time! Wesley's meeting with God that evening not only changed a disillusioned missionary into a man of conviction but it spearheaded a religious and social revolution in the eighteenth century and led to millions sharing that life-changing event. The testimonies of the young man and John Wesley are, of course, common to the great evangelical tradition where commitment to the Christian revelation is said to be sealed through a heart experience of God's love and his forgiveness through the cross.

A fourth type we might call "encounter" experiences which focus on ways in which people encounter the "otherness", the "numinous", the "mysteriousness" of God. Two influential thinkers, Martin Buber, a Jewish philosopher, and Rudolph Otto, a German protestant theologian, have shown how prevalent is the experience of meeting God in human life. It may happen through what Otto called the experience of *mysterium tremendum* by which he meant an experience of God through nature, in art and so on, where feelings of awe and wonder may be compared to Moses' encounter with God at the burning bush. Or a meeting with God might come in a mystical experience leading to a realisation of the holiness and majesty of Almighty God. A well-documented testimony down the Christian centuries, of course. But it might, conceivably, come through the intervention of God at points of despair, illness and even at the point of death. Experiences of healing are seen by many as direct intervention by a creator God who has revealed himself personally and lovingly in some specific way. Those of us with extensive pastoral experience do not need to be reminded of the frequency of such claims and, interestingly, it often happens to those outside the formal structures of the Christian faith as well as to those within it.

Finally, we must point to that "experience" of even more people which is the quiet testimony of God's providential dealings with them in life. They may have encountered tragedy, difficulty and pain (indeed, often such ingredients are part of the testimony itself) and they point to God's hand in delivering them or interpreting the pain or problem. While this is scarcely "experience" in a direct way – indeed, some believers might be reticent about claiming it as an experience at all – it is experience of a faith which is for them authentic and relevant. The ordered world of daily business, family life and daily prayer, the influence of impressive Christian living by others, the importance of the sacraments in worship and so on, are contexts in which such people find God's presence in their lives. For such people there is hardly a need for extraordinary interventions because God is with them all the time.

We must however at this point make a most important observation. The character of Christian experience of God is much more than that certain individuals have had experiences of him. The Church itself is founded upon the experience of those who have met God and whose lives have been changed as a result. It is highly doubtful that there would have been such an institution as the Church if the first disciples had not witnessed the resurrection and believed down to the last fibre of their beings that they had met God. It is furthermore extremely unlikely that Saul the Rabbi would have given up such an interesting and career-fulfilling occupation as persecuting Christians unless a real event – for him – on the Damascus road had not put an end to it and led him outside the Establishment of his day. It is highly doubtful, also, if the missionary enterprise of the Church down the ages would have got off the ground at all if the saints, martyrs and missionaries had not experienced their own sense of God's personal "call". All these experiences and many more beside can hardly be shrugged off as irrelevant to our quest for God. Indeed, experience we have to grant is at the heart of the Christian faith. To know God is to know him, not as an article in the creed, but as a real person. If, then, God is real and is the One behind all things that are, we are not surprised to hear a testimony rising from the hearts of many people that he does disclose himself and the hem of his garment may be touched. And we must be clear about that – that is all that such experiences are. No experience of God is really a revealing of the whole God in all his splendour and majesty. At the best we catch but glimpses of his nature and grace.

But how do we test the reality of such experiences?

What **are** we to make of such claims? We must obviously start with the character of the person who is claiming an experience of meeting God. Who is this person who tells me of the God he has encountered? Is she a person I respect and trust? Does the testimony ring true to what I know of her, her intellect, moral standing, temperament and character? The more sane, rational and well known to me an individual is, the more likely I am to accept what she has to say. I may not be prepared to believe yet what she believes, or to follow her way, but I will not be able to deny that for her the experience of knowing God has resulted in something which has challenged her previous way of handling life and challenges mine as well. What I will not be able to get at will be the actual experience itself – but, as we acknowledged earlier, that is true of any personal claim or conviction whether it be religious or secular. What I can do is view that experience in the context of this person's life. If a basically sane and rational man or woman whose life and character is invariably well-integrated actually claims to have had such an experience, then I may be impressed and even deeply disconcerted – and may have to revise my ideas about God and how he works.

Second, we must apply the test of moral consequences. If someone claims to have experienced the living God we will not expect them to carry on as if it is of no significance. We will want to ask: "What difference has it made to his life?" For example, some years ago I had as a student a most interesting man who became a Christian in prison. This man, David, was sentenced to ten years for a serious kidnapping offence. He was a very nasty customer. In prison he was brought to his senses through the break-up of his marriage, a realisation of the stupidity of his life and its lack of moral direction. Over a period of time he opened his mind and heart to God. One evening, the culmination of many months of discussing and arguing with a prison visitor, he cried out in despair in the quietness of his cell: "I am hopeless, rotten and in need. If you are real, God, reveal yourself to me". That was the turning point, David was to say later, and he quietly claims that God met him that night in a personal way that made him a different man. There was nothing spectacular about this, but there is little doubt that for David it was a life-changing event which has made the most profound difference to his life. And this is what we should expect if an experience of meeting God is real – it will result in a changed life, in different habits and life style.

So, we might say, one way of checking the truth or falsity of such claims to have "seen", "met", or "heard" God is by what we may call a "reality check" on the lives of those who make such statements about claims to know God. While a person's more sceptical friends may doubt the value of his arguments about the truth of the Christian faith, the REALITY of his faith and his testimony to the power of God in his life will not be something they can quickly ignore or reject.

Nevertheless it must be concluded that experience itself is not a conclusive argument for the existence of God. That is not what I am arguing. After all, there are people of other faiths or none at all who have had mystical experiences and we can't all be right! And of course, a Christian would not want to claim that religious experience solves all the problems in one go. We do not see experience standing on its own in any sense. Experience must have the support of argument if it is to convince. Just as faith without works is dead so experience without a strong grounding in a biblical faith, together with a rational framework, is dead also. The value of experience for many people is twofold; firstly, it re-orders into a coherent whole what up to now in a person's life has been disparate and unorganized. It is the testimony of many a person that through the experience of meeting God, what his heart and mind have been seeking and yearning for for years, is what he has found.

Secondly, experience we must clearly understand is not a special kind of truth, nor is religious experience a queer, unnatural kind of experience belonging to some strange and other world. Experience of God is encountered in ordinary life and we may describe it as ordinary experience understood at full depth. What makes that truth religious is not that it relates to some abnormal field of thought and feeling but that it goes to the very root of the experience which it interprets. T. S. Eliot's evocative words, "We had the experience but missed the meaning" goes to the very centre of modern life. Openness to God enables the ordinary experiences of life to become fully impregnated with meaning and divine reality.

Experience, then, undergirds faith and reason. It can never replace them. But for the person who up to now has been reflecting on the Christian faith, the invitation comes, "to taste and see that the Lord is good". There can be no denying that the variegated experiences of God are powerful challenges to modern secular people whose philosophy of "seeing is believing" is confounded by a form of experiencing which has had such a powerful influence upon people down the centuries and still continues to do so today.

8

The Case against Unbelief

We said at the beginning of the book that faith is not given a real opportunity in Western culture to present its case for a living and loving God because the entire weight of opinion and culture stifles its voice and does not pay heed to its message. The confident message that comes across is that Christianity is discredited and that, regretfully, its story belongs to the past along with other myths of perfection and life everlasting. We are being robbed of a chance to discover the reality of a firm faith in God and of encountering him as Creator and Friend. But, really, is it a fact that faith has had its day?

If that is the case we have to ask why it has persisted in maintaining a stubborn presence in the Marxist-Leninist culture of Russia, China and other places where deliberate attempts have been made to squeeze it out of existence. Indeed, its resurgence in places where atheistic communism has suppressed Christianity for decades is an impressive story. And it is a matter of wonder that it still continues to exist and flourish in the sophisticated, technological cultures of the West where, although leaner and slimmer since Christianity has separated from its secular culture, it is perhaps more effective than it has ever been because of its stand upon issues of morality and value, matters which continue to meet an echo in the aspirations of modern people.

It is my conviction that rather than faith in a personal God being intellectually discredited the reverse is the case. It is not that modern science has found Christian belief to be lacking an intellectual basis, but rather when all the facts are considered together we begin to see atheism, unbelief and materialism as the imposters they are. In this chapter I want to explore the serious weaknesses of atheistic materialism and to show that far from presenting a threat to faith, the questions it cannot answer tip the balance in favour of the hypothesis of God.

Firstly, materialism is UNCONVINCING. We are asked to believe that sheer chance brought the entire universe into existence. We are also told that we must not posit the existence of a personal God because that hypothesis is unprovable anyway. Instead we are exhorted to marvel at the great god "Chance" who created all things. But when the facts are considered together we have grounds to be sceptical of such a theory. Let us look at the evidence. We are asked to believe that a totally random event, the famous "Big Bang", created the universe as we know it which led to the creation of matter and time. We are asked further to accept another thesis that, unplanned, out of the primeval soup of amino acids, organic life emerged and, millions of years later, intelligent life appeared.

In the last decade or so scientists have taken a special interest in chance and have applied scientific data to the laws of probability – the results to date have shaken scientific thinking. Professor Bartholomew of London University asks, for example, how order can arise out of primeval chaos when the stream of development is running in the opposite direction. That is to say, when chaos is supposed to have been the original characteristic of primeval creation it is surprising that conditions to support life emerged. He and many other scientists have shown that rather than order arising by "accident" from chaos, it was there in the first place; that the distribution of gas in the universe from the "big bang" had to be delicately and precisely balanced to produce galaxies; and that even an error of minute proportions $(1:10^{40})$ would have destroyed life. We are left therefore startled at the "miracle" of this chance event. Bartholomew wonders whether this suggests rather that "there must have been a deliberate input of information at an early stage which served as a programme (in the computing sense) to engineer the highly-structured world we live in".

A similar problem emerges from the chance of life starting from the primeval soup of amino acids which are thought to be at the origin of life. We are told that over a period of billions of years the random mixing of these acids spontaneously generated life. Most of us happily accept these facts because the information comes to us with the *imprimatur* of science assuring us that the facts are infallibly correct. Yet the odds against this happening of its own volition are simply huge. Hoyle and Wickramasinghe have postulated that the probability of creating 2,000 highly complex enzymes from random combinations of amino acids is infinitesimal. Hoyle likens it to the same odds as throwing an uninterrupted sequence of 50,000 sixes with unbiased dice. Sure, it could happen over millions of years but the odds involved are simply fantastic. And all this, mind you, precedes the astonishing appearance of intelligent life on an obscure little planet in the backwaters of the universe.

However, it is important not to overplay the argument from probability. Bartholomew in a restrained and considered essay subjects the hypothesis of Hoyle and Wickramasinghe to critical analysis and shows that such enormous odds quoted do not prove God beyond reasonable doubt. And this is quite true. All it reveals is the staggering odds involved in postulating intelligent life originating spontaneously without the direct will of a creator. But what is significant is that the case for materialism, resting as it does on random happenings, on unintelligent and accidental causes, has now to face the fact that the odds of the world we know and intelligent life emerging are overwhelmingly huge. Consider the implications of the remarks of the scientist Mark Doughty who explains that in the very first milliseconds after the original explosion there must have been present all the conditions for life on our seemingly insignificant planet, including the self-directed and self-conscious form of life which we call human, and that our human brains were encoded in certain minute atomic data present at the dawn of time. Little wonder that the idea of a creator who planned the universe seems to most people to be more plausible than a materialistic explanation. The philosopher Swinburne comments with some force: "It is very unlikely that a universe would exist uncaused but rather more likely that God would exist uncaused". For Swinburne, and many of us, the explanation of the universe is made more puzzling, not less, by the denial of a personal creator.

Secondly, materialism is UNLIKELY. Let me use a rather rough analogy. If I were told that the first typewriter was, in fact, not the product of intelligence but fashioned haphazardly and randomly by forces of nature, in which the different parts came together over millions of years – each piece undesigned, and undifferentiated – finally arriving at comprising a product which is intelligible, some credulity would be required for us to accept this idea which goes completely against our experience of life. We would marvel at such a process and probably suspect the presence of a mind to bring this about. Of course, we are not opposed to the idea of evolution over millions of years. Most of us accept that hypothesis. But what I am sceptical of is the suggestion that random events can produce the order we know to be a reality of the structure of things. And let us make no mistake about it, as we argued earlier, the very order of the universe is such an overwhelming fact that it not only creates the possibility for knowledge and science but also that it is part of the condition of an intelligent universe. As Professor Farmer put it so splendidly years ago: "It is only because the fire can be relied on to boil the kettle, and the sound waves to carry our speech, that we can indulge in that highly personal activity called a tea-party".

What we are arguing here is for continuity between the universe and ourselves. For the materialist, intelligence, consciousness, illusions of freedom and so on are but the epiphenemenon that is a by-product of life. They have no existence apart from us and are but accidental additions which have arisen by good fortune. This suggestion, with whatever sophistication it is expressed, is DESPERATE, because to be convincing it has to deny not only our experience of life – which we assume to be logical and intelligent – but it also has to sever consciousness and intelligence from life by making them elements which are by-products of impersonal and mechanistic forces; they are merely the concomitants of certain types of organic life. They exist in us and nowhere else. But we have to ask with the Catholic philosopher Lonergan, how is it that this world and all we experience may be interpreted by intelligence if it does not have an intelligent basis? How curious it is that in all our exploring, searching and struggling we find that our minds meet a Mind. The physicist David Bohm came to the conclusion that materialism left more questions unanswered than it solved and remarked: "When I see the immense order of the universe (and especially the brain of man) I cannot escape feeling that this ground unfolds supreme intelligence. And although this is not quite so evident, I would say that this intelligence is permeated with compassion and love."

Thirdly, materialism is LIMITING. Exclude God from life and allow that all morality and standards of value are relative because God is not, and the result is not greater freedom for mankind but a fresh bondage because our spirits are now chained. The irony is that we need God to be fully human. Materialism, instead of revealing the true character of life, obscures it because it mistakes mystery for superstition. But mystery is necessary if humankind is to grow to its full stature. Strangely enough, science and philosophy are beginning to acknowledge that the only way we can have a true and full understanding of the universe is in terms of analogy, metaphor, poetry and sometimes paradox. Niels Bohr, the eminent quantum physicist, is forced, for example, in his discipline to resort to metaphor when he describes scientific truth in the following way: "When it comes to atoms, language can be used only as in poetry. The poet (like the quantum physicist) is concerned with creating images and establishing connections . . . Quantum theory provides us with a striking illustration of the fact that we can fully understand a connection though we can only speak of it in images and parables."

But scientists, in drawing upon metaphor and poetry to describe things that are beyond sensory perception are also being compelled to reject a materialism which was at the heart of a nineteenth-century philosophy of science. David Bohm argues that it is a mistake to regard the elemental particles of matter as "things" which collectively make up bigger things. This "building block" method is dismissed. Rather we should think of the world as a "network of relations". Our experience of it may be as a collection of "things" but to the quantum scientist it is an integrated web of energy patterns in which nothing is independent. Bohm is led to the conclusion that, "The implicate order implies a reality immensely beyond matter. Matter itself is merely a ripple in this background – and the ocean of energy is not primarily in space or time at all". This way of looking at reality opens up the one-dimensional universe of materialism and makes it possible for us to see the wonderful mystery of life and the way that science, art, philosophy, poetry and human living, each has its part to play in illuminating life and its richness. Professor Stuart Hampshire similarly attacks materialism for its reductionism: "Materialism is wrong because it does not do justice to the mental life in terms of imagination, belief, and memory and to its social implications".

It is this rejection of a cosmic Mind and of a divine

purpose that is at the heart of materialism. For many
decades it has reigned supreme because it seems so
completely and literally "sensible". There does not seem
to be any real reason to go beyond the evidences of the
physical world to explain the whole of reality. But these
days there are very few physicists who would claim to
be clear materialists or empiricists. The reason for this
is twofold. The first has to do with the nature of reality. We no longer believe in the old "billiard ball" idea
of nature but in a complex structure of things which
make the older way of seeing things difficult to accept
today. The mechanical world of Newtonian physics –
according to which all things that exist are physical
things with a distinct reality, however small they may
be – gave way to an Einsteinian universe in which this
description was abandoned. Leptons, quarks, muons
and photons are not pieces of matter in any imaginable
sense. Eddington used to give an example of the two
different approaches when in lectures he spoke of his
two tables. The first was solid, brown, three feet high
and rectangular and quite obviously visible. The other
was mostly space with here and there some mysterious
entity which had to be imagined at one moment as a
wave and at another as a particle. As Eddington made
clear, these did not represent two different tables but
the same reality – and both were correct from different
perceptions. In short the great attraction of materialism
led to its downfall. It appeared to be the case that the
only fundamental properties of the structure of things
are mass, position and velocity. But modern physics
have not so much destroyed the old mechanistic view
of the universe as have made it seem too superficial.
We now see the universe as a vastly more mysterious

and complex entity than the former "billiard ball" view of things.

The second reason has to do with the way that materialism separates life into two great compartments. The first is the physical world; cold, indifferent and hostile to mankind. The second is the world of culture and life we create to sustain ourselves which is warm, friendly and meaningful up to a point. Quite obviously the disjuncture of these two realities reveals a failure on the part of materialism to give a real basis for human life, values and morals but given its starting point how can it relate the two worlds if the former is the harsh reality of all things and the latter the accidental by-product of impersonal forces in nature? So it appears that such forms of materialism are unsatisfactory because they open up a chasm between life of the world and human culture and aspirations. A coherent philosophy and science must do justice to both worlds.

Fourthly, materialistic atheism is UNSATISFACTORY IN ITS UNDERSTANDING OF VALUE. We all know the problem of evil for the Christian. Our chapter earlier did not minimise the questions posed by affirming God's love which is daily challenged by disasters and events which ask us what God is doing. But by focussing the searchlight on the believer, the person who rejects God may be oblivious of the uncomfortable questions which search him out, perhaps even more rigorously. First, there is the fact as we noticed earlier that, prevalent as evil most certainly is in the world, who needs convincing that the presence of good far outweighs the element of evil. Harmony, peace, goodness, hope, joy and love are the basic constituents of life more than evil, destruction and death. Such realities are the bases of the great civilisations; they flood our literature and illuminate our homes and lives; they give meaning and stability.

Further, if there is no God, no final explanation of this world, it is encumbent upon us to explain the problem of good in a godless world. Adolph Deissmann once remarked: "You should never take anything away from a person unless you can give him something better". We are still awaiting this better world-view from the non-believer. How do we reconcile with a blind, indifferent and irrational cosmos, the discovery of truth, beauty and the power of sacrificial love? The majority of us just cannot accept the notion that such virtues are culturally formed and governed. Whether we are practising Christians or not the presence of moral values and human values of grace and dignity are seen by many of us as pointing beyond us to a "Something" or "Someone" who transcends us and calls us to a "divinity" we do not as yet possess. Our god-idea is the acid test of our valuation of life. As we saw earlier the moral framework of life is shattered or severely weakened when the faith around it, on which it was built, is destroyed. Atheism destroys the basis of any kind of moral certainty. But when we take the issue of freedom the atheist is particularly vulnerable. It is a feature of existential atheism to reject God, on the one hand, to make room for human freedom on the belief that the existence of God destroys the autonomy and freedom of mankind. Yet, on the other hand, the same philosophy will reject belief in God because he does not intervene to rescue the victims of human villainy! Atheists cannot have it both ways.

But let us go deeper into this question of value. It is of course possible for the unbeliever to argue that our total concepts of morality and human goodness are but the random products of physical events, that claims of religious experience are illusory and that humankind's pleasure in art, music and things of the spirit do not point beyond him but come from his deepest aspirations only, but the net result is to take from life the very things that give to it its significance and meaning. So the writer Philip Toynbee comments: "What I would say is that if it were irrefutably demonstrated to me that there is no God, and no reality above or distinct from the material world, then I would consider that human life is too terrible to be endured. Fear and some regard for the feelings of others might prevent me killing myself but I would live out my life as a prisoner." Toynbee is there giving expression to feelings that many of us have about the value of the transcendent in life. It is not that God is called upon to be a Father-substitute to face a hostile world but that we perceive that we cannot conceive of morality and such values as freedom, love, peace and hope without addressing a Being who gives these qualities their authentication. The position of the theist is that in moral awareness and the growth of conscience we trace the mark of God the creator who has created us in such a way that we are aware of what a good and loving way is to live and to behave. We call these discoveries "moral disclosures" because they point from us to a God who has made us in his image and likeness.

Enough has been written in this chapter to suggest that the Christian concept of a personal God is superior to ideas which reject him. I believe strongly that belief in a personal God has advantages over agnosticism and atheism in the following respects:

1. By believing in the existence of a rational and personal creator we have a more *comprehensive* picture of the universe. It is a universe with a purposeful and loving creator who is working out his plan for all things in the vicissitudes and trials of life. A non-theistic explanation, as we have seen, has the difficulty of explaining how order came from disorder (if that is the case) and, if order was the primary reality, how that came into existence. Agnosticism only projects its agnosticism further back. More questions have to be answered if God is rejected. A theistic explanation does not believe that agnosticism is justified and suggests that the most reasonable hypothesis is that the primary reality is a creator God who has brought all things into being.

2. We argue, furthermore, that theism is a more simple and satisfactory explanation. We are used to making and creating things and it is reasonable to deduce that, in a world in which order and causality reign, a personal act willed that the universe should have this character. Although this explanation is simple and straightforward, the understanding of reality and the way it takes us into analogy, metaphor and mystery is far from being simplistic. The history of Christian thought is a sufficient denial of the idea that to be a Christian believer means crucifying one's intellect. On the contrary, such a faith integrates knowledge and experience; it awakens awe, mystery and wonder which are at the heart of being a human being.

3. The presence of a personal creator makes sense of our place in the scheme of things and unites the world of nature and humankind which atheism divides. Instead of seeing ourselves as exceptional beings, creatures curiously and inextricably thrown up by chance in a mysterious cosmos, we see the unity of everything and in this way can see the principle of morality which stands over us and which beckons us to fullness of life. The statement of the scientist, Freeman Dyson, quoted earlier, that "the universe in some sense must have known we were coming", coincides with the Christian conviction that this created order is truly our home and the place where we meet God.

9

What Kind of God?

We have seen that there are reasonable grounds for postulating the existence of a Being who has created all things. Some people, however, want us to stop there with an unknowable, ultimately mysterious divinity who is inaccessible to us. They remind us of the vastness of this wonderful universe and tell us that such immensities mock our feeble attempts to communicate with the creator. We must go no further, they tell us. We must live with mystery. "Yes, we grant that the clues for the existence of God are strong but nothing more can be said. Be content with the little we know."

We can make two responses to this call for agnosticism immediately. Firstly, it hardly seems logical to make the vastness of the universe an obstacle to God communicating his essence to us. To affirm that God exists is to say, as we have pointed out, that this universe is not a product of blind chance but is controlled by an intelligent purpose. It does not make sense therefore to say he exists but that he has no plans for us and he keeps himself aloof from his creation. If he is able to contemplate the great details of creation he is surely able to give personal attention to the intimate details of life. It follows from the nature of a supreme being that it is precisely because he is supreme that he is able to care about small things. We reduce God to our likeness when we doubt his power to reveal himself.

Of course we should realise that God in his essence is ultimately beyond our full understanding. We talk about God as "he" but must appreciate that such language is only analogical. God is "wholly other" and when the Bible uses the masculine pronoun "he", and when it also uses both masculine and feminine attributes to describe God, it is unlikely that even for the writers of sacred literature such terminology was intended to be taken as literally true. This is to say then that such images must not be taken literally as suggesting that God is "male". Whatever we say about the creator only approximates to "his" nature. "We see through a glass darkly" is true of all Christian thought. Though we may be confident about our knowledge of God, his greatness is ultimately beyond our thinking and conceiving. Perhaps we in the West, then, need to learn from the tradition of Eastern Othodoxy which approaches the mystery of God by the way of negativity in order to understand the wonder of the One who has given us life. This *via negativa* starts by saying what God is not, in order to arrive at what he is for us. Sometimes called "kataphatic" theology, the method of the East moves from negation to a cautious knowledge of God who is unchanging, not limited, all-loving and so on. This type of approach is caught beautifully in the poet R. S. Thomas's description of God:

> Why no! I never thought other than
> That God is the great absence
> In our lives, the empty silence
> Within, the place where we go
> Seeking, not in hope to

Arrive or find.
He keeps the interstices
In our knowledge, the darkness
Between stars.
His are the echoes
We follow, the footprints he has
just Left.

This stance, which starts with the greatness of God,
is a healthy corrective to the confident assumptions of
the tradition of Western Christianity which has often too
brashly assumed that God's nature is self-evident and
that we can make clear dogmatic statements about him.
The danger of this approach (which has been called the
"apophatic" tradition), is that we make God into an object
of knowledge and lose sight of his majesty and awesome
might. Nevertheless, a balanced idea of God will contain
both these emphases; we do exist in God and his world
and we shall never in this life ever be able to penetrate
beyond the outer courtyard of knowledge, but he is still
a Father, friend and redeemer to those who trust him.

If our first response to agnosticism, then, must spring
from our understanding of God's ability to give attention to everything, always and all at once, the second
response must flow from the character of God as one
whose nature is always to give. Revelation springs from
"giving". To give is to reveal what was formerly hidden.
We have many illustrations of this from everyday life.
When someone gives himself or herself to me in acts of
sacrifice, generosity and love, something new is shared
which comes with the gift which is a revelation of the
love-gift. Similarly, by creating, God pours his very
self into his creation and comes to us. This means

that the creator has made it possible for us to receive
these intimations of the divine. The Jewish theologian
J. Neusner speaks splendidly of "man's walled mind
which has no access to a ladder upon which he can,
on his own strength, rise to knowledge of God. Yet his
soul is endowed with translucent windows that open to
the beyond." Even though Christian theology correctly
questions humankind's ability to discern fully the work
of God in his world through our fallenness, yet we are
not always blind to the wonder of his works or deaf to
his call. Some of us have experienced those moments of
translucence when we have caught a glimpse of the beauty of nature with such intensity that we have wanted to
exclaim with Gerard Hopkins, "the world is charged with
the grandeur of God!" Hopkins' poem goes on to affirm
the "dearest, freshness deep down things" of God's creation. For others the awareness of the spiritual has come
through the awesome media of music, poetry or art. In
a million different ways the giving of God goes on and
our antennae have the ability to pick up the signals of
a universal God who reveals himself in the music and
poetry of creation. It is no accident, then, that we can
"hear" the language of God because the facility has been
given to us.

We can go much further than that. We have to say
that a Christian is not a philosopher who has found a
satisfactory theory of the universe but is someone who
believes in a personal God. One cannot pray to an
abstraction but only to a person. So, the cry of the
Christian thinker Paul Claudel on the evening of his
conversion to the Christian faith as he stood by a pillar
in the cathedral of Notre Dame: "Lord, all of a sudden
you have become for me a person!" Christians are not

people who have discovered a useful world-view, or an interesting and absorbing philosophy, or a caring life-style – although we would submit that it is all and more of these things. Christians are a body of followers of Jesus Christ who have life, hope and purpose through him. He is alive and lives in them.

If, in creating, the giving of God is known we also find in this giving a self-limitation on the part of God. It is normal in Christian theology to talk about God as omniscient and omnipotent. But is he in fact all powerful? This traditional way of talking about God hardly makes sense when full rein is given to the fact of his self-giving. By creating individuals with free will, God himself is limited by his act of creation; he chooses to be diminished in order for us to grow. We do not diminish him but he freely and deliberately enters upon a process of self-emptying (kenosis) and refrains from using his power. He creates a world in which we have freedom to grow; a freedom that entails the risk that part of his creation may reject him, abuse his freedom, exploit his world, and even usurp the powers of the Creator. So close is divinisation and demonisation; the brave new world so quickly becomes the killing fields of man's greed and hatred.

It is because of this link between God's self-giving and self-limitation that I for one am grateful for the insights of a theological movement known as "process theology". Two thinkers in particular have popularized this new way of looking at God's ways with his creation – the mathematician Alfred Whitehead and the philosopher Charles Hartshorne. Process theology rejects the idea of God as being totally "outside time" and as an immutable Being – that is, unchangeable in his nature.

They accuse traditional theology of failing to do justice to the rich Biblical portrait of God who suffers with his creation and they charge it with absorbing concepts of an unchanging God which owe more to Greek thought than Christian ideas. Process thought sees the whole of creation as being "in process" with God being immanent and transcendent. In his immanence God works within the processes of creation and to some degree is subject to the laws which are fundamental to its existence. Thus in contrast with traditional views of God which see him outside events, process theology envisages the Creator as being in a continual state of interaction with life, even to the degree of being influenced by events.

There is much that is attractive about process thought. It makes sense of a world which is plainly in process. "The whole creation groans in travail until now" is how St Paul saw a universe on its way to full redemption (Romans 8). The same passage shows God's close involvement with his creation in suffering with it and caring for it and bringing it to eventual re-birth. Process theology is coherent in speaking of a Creator so intimately associated with his workmanship that he is also affected by it. He takes suffering and change into himself and transforms them into hopeful possibilities of growth. From this perspective evil itself can be considered even redemptive because if God is in the processes of life and is affected by them, nothing is totally and irredeemably evil. Such a description of God in relation to his world is surely deeply Christian. God remains God but always with his creation, rejoicing in its achievements and suffering from its failures. A Christianity with its doctrine of incarnation will identify with any doctrine of God which "earths" him in the reality of the world.

There are several aspects of process theology, however, which makes me hesitate in embracing it wholeheartedly. There is on the one hand a tendency on the part of some process theologians to create a philosophy of process thought which has but tenuous connections with Christian thought. Thus Whitehead's model of God with its "primordial" and "consequent" poles which is his attempt to replace the classical modes of immanence and transcendence is scarcely obvious. On what basis do we reject the one as being non-Christian and yet accept the other? But more seriously, so completely does this theology subsume God within his creation that it appears to make him a creature of time and seemingly impotent to deal with the problems of life. The problem then for process theology appears to be that of its failure to balance immanence with the transcendence of God. Unless God is seen as standing outside the structures of creation as well as being fully involved in the structures we will end up with a God who is imprisoned by his own laws.

Nevertheless, process thought is right in what it affirms of God's involvement in life and this concept of God is thoroughly Biblical and takes us directly into the character of God as revealed by scripture. In defining what God is like, the Bible gives us many possible answers which range from his transcendence over all things as a loving Creator to the one who comes to us in humility in a human life. Now, although the Bible is, for the Christian, God's clearest testimony of who he is and what he demands from us, it is also the record of humankind's search for God and his gradual self-revelation. We find in the Old Testament, for example, men and women groping beyond themselves for the divine and finding him little by little. To a great extent the picture of God developed as people discovered him and as he made them his people. Indeed, there is a curious overlapping of revelation and searching. The knowledge of God came from God's side as he allowed his people to see different facets of his character. Yet from another point of view, they "discovered" him as their pilgrimage continued. Through the **acts** of God they found the true God. So Abraham is led out by the Unknown into a new land and each act of faith is rewarded by fresh revelations of the One who goes before.

Similarly, the events which betook the Hebrew tribes in Egypt and their subsequent escape proceed from their risk of faith and lead them into knowledge of the One who declares himself to be *Yahweh*, the One who is Eternal yet ever present. The high point of knowledge of God is found in the great prophetic tradition which finds its peak in Isaiah, Jeremiah, Hosea and Amos. Here God is splendidly depicted as the Creator of all things, the One who has no rival. Isaiah supplies the grandeur of a lofty deity, Jeremiah the highly personal qualities of One who cares, whilst Hosea and Amos add the ingredient that such a God makes ethical demands upon people that coincide with his character as one who loves, who is pure and holy.

The New Testament does not contradict the development of the Old Testament but it does add something quite unusual, controversial and for the Christian, wonderful, namely that the human face of God is Jesus Christ. He, claims the New Testament, is the way to the Father.

But did Jesus himself make this claim? The answer

appears somewhat ambiguous when we go directly to the earliest gospels written. The Synoptic gospels, that is, Matthew, Mark and Luke, reveal a reticence on the part of Jesus to be explicit about himself and his mission. Jesus makes few claims for himself but draws them from his disciples. "Who do people say I am?" drew various responses from his followers. "Some say you are a prophet, even as great as Elijah." And then the swift counterpunch: "And what about you? Who do you think I am?" This evoked Simon Peter's famous confession: "You are the Christ (Messiah), the Son of the Living God." It is arguably the case that although this confession was a watershed in the disciples' understanding of Jesus, uncertainty and mystery still clouded him. It was not until after his death and resurrection that clarity came concerning him.

But at this point we must say a word about the character of the gospels. They are not biographies as we know the meaning of that term. They do not purport to be objective accounts of the course of this amazing man's career, from birth to death. Rather they are "confessional" material, written from the viewpoint of writers who have been profoundly influenced by his life and teaching. They have already reached conclusions about Jesus and want others to know him too. This does not mean that we cannot trust the material given to us in the gospels. Far from it, they give us a first-century account of the impact he made on the lives of many. What we cannot escape as we read the gospels is the directness of Jesus. His personality comes across. There is a "ring of truth" about the writings as J. B. Phillips so aptly put it. They show his humanness, his growth, his struggles and the opposition to him, as the popular preacher from Nazareth reveals his identity as stemming from One who sent him to preach the Kingdom of God.

Yet even if Jesus did not directly claim to be "God" the evidence is clear enough to show that his teaching, miracles and lifestyle confronted people with the divine. Men and women found themselves groping beyond words to describe him. And the death of this unusual preacher from Nazareth did not stem the stories and the arguments. Whatever we might say about the resurrection, "something" happened which turned frightened men into bold disciples; which created the Christian church; which made devout Jews turn their Sabbath from a Saturday to a Sunday; which made the Jews turf the Christians out of their synagogues; and which gave birth to the New Testament. Even today, the story continues of people finding that Jesus Christ is far more than a historical figure. He leaps from the pages of the New Testament; from the testimony of the church; from the testimony of his followers – into the lives of all who seek genuinely his truth.

The rest of the New Testament continues the amazing story of Jesus. The first Christians from the very beginning made startling claims for their leader, taking over terms from Jewish and Greek sources that might resonate meaning for their hearers. Claims are now made of him which approximate to statements made of Almighty God. He is called "Lord", a term commonly used of a divine being. Other descriptions reveal the estimate that was given to his significance: Wisdom, Life, the Way and even the "visible of the Invisible God". Thomas in the fourth gospel falls at the feet of the Risen Christ and calls him "My Lord and my God" because the good news of Christianity calls men and women to meet the Living

God and this they do when they meet the One who was sent.

At this point we meet what theologians call the "scandal of particularity". That is, Christianity makes the bold claim that Jesus Christ is so incomparable that we meet God fully in him. In this particular man, God is known. This does not mean of course that God cannot be known in other faiths. Mainstream Christianity treats other religions with respect and allows that God can be known, and is known by men and women of non-Christian faiths. We do not deny that in the higher religions of mankind there are glimpses of the divine. But we cannot shift from the conviction that is as old as the New Testament that God is revealed FULLY AND FINALLY in the person of Jesus Christ. We know how infuriating and arrogant such a claim must seem to those who sincerely believe that in their scriptures and in their worship God is found and experienced. But we have to say with Paul as he preached to the adherents of other faiths in Athens: "What you worship but do not know – this is what I now proclaim" (Acts 17:23). This scandal of particularity we must live with. Christians cannot yield this un-negotiable element in their faith. We believe that the God of the universe longs to reveal himself and he does in many different ways and forms, through religion, through reason, art and human intelligence but each and every one of these ways is limited. Only in a personal relationship with the living God experienced in Jesus Christ can he be known.

10

What Kind of Response?

Bishop Edward Barnes, once a famous mathematician and Bishop of Birmingham concluded his Gifford Lectures with these words: "I too have realized how vast is our ignorance of the world in which we find ourselves and to which we belong. Can it be, I am compelled to ask, that with such a feeling of ignorance I shall pass to a realm where knowledge is not, because consciousness has ceased? Must we allow that the desire to understand God's works and ways, which is one of the strongest and purest of human passions, is a vain and hopeless by-product of man's search for material comfort? Do we but rise for a moment above the waters of unconsciousness and, after a brief glance around, sink again to eternal oblivion? If such is indeed our fate, then surely the mystery of human life is unfathomable; unreason must sit enthroned above meaningless chance. Now I for one cannot believe that within a few years my brief attempt to understand the universe will have ceased".

Dr Barnes' conviction is, of course, shared by this writer and by many millions of thinking Christians and adherents of other faiths. And this conviction comes, as Dr Barnes makes clear, in spite of the fact that we are ignorant about so much of the universe, the world, human nature and God himself. The vastness of our ignorance does not paralyse our endeavours to know, neither does it make us lose confidence in the comparatively little we do know. The question that remains is: Do we know enough for us to place our confidence in the Christian faith?

Before we tackle that question directly a number of other matters should be cleared out of the way. Firstly, the Christian explanation of life does not necessarily replace other ways of looking at the world. That is to say, a scientist is not forced to abandon a scientific way of considering the objective realities all around. Neither for that matter is the artist or the businessman forced to adopt a completely different world-view once he has become a Christian. The search for truth in a thoroughly disinterested way is, I want to insist, at the very heart of a Christian faith which claims Jesus Christ to be the Way, the Truth and the Life. If he is the Truth then no mature Christian will want to stand in the way of scientific investigation. Indeed, true faith and true knowledge walk arm in arm towards the goal of total knowledge. What this suggests is that life has many different layers which contribute towards the Christian idea of reality. It is when one of these is seen as the exclusive vehicle of knowledge that error and distortion set in. Classic examples of this spring instantly to mind. There was for example the regrettable error of the Roman Catholic church in the seventeenth century when it demanded from Galileo a retraction of his thesis that the earth revolves around the sun. Galileo did so reluctantly because his life was threatened although we understand that he muttered just loud enough for his friends to hear: "The earth goes around the sun, just the same!" Similarly, in the last century the church in this land made a fool of itself by attacking the theory of evolution because it mistakenly believed that the Genesis account was a literal account. Today, the hypothesis of evolution is accepted readily by most of us, Christians as well as non-Christians.

But it is not only Christians who lapse into a one-dimensional view of the world. In philosophy the idea associated with A. J. Ayer, that we can only really know things which are appropriated by our senses, is an outdated theory because this is palpably not the case. How deficient human life would be if this became the touchstone of reality, but as we are aware such a perception only covers the peripheral aspects of life. And, no doubt, we can all think of other examples of a rigid attitude to life, reality and knowledge, which by ignoring other aspects represents a distorted view of knowledge. No, such unbalanced emphases fail to make sense of the wholeness of life. And it is this element of wholeness which is a feature of a balanced Christianity when faith in God complements and draws together other forms of knowledge. I have been impressed by the significant number of scientists who have said to me that finding God has for them made sense of the data they work with daily. Somehow an awareness of a personal and loving God has become a unitive factor in their knowledge and scientific study.

Secondly we must say something about "needing God". It is sometimes said that the presence of religion in the world – which even the most jaundiced agnostic will admit to be extremely prevalent in human history and shows no sign of diminishing – is merely a psychological crutch which reassures insecure people that they are not alone. This way of explaining religion which started with Feuerbach, journeyed into Marxism, was continued by Freud and has become folklore with some sophisticates, should be dismissed by all thinking people. To be sure, there will always be those who will need crutches and a faith supplies this for some. But for the vast majority of Christians such a suggestion is an insult and an inadequate explanation for the presence of faith in God.

On the contrary, a number of things can be said about need. We can say with Philip Toynbee, the journalist, for example, that "It is true that the need is no proof that God exists; but it is at least a suggestive and interesting element in many people's composition. Strange creatures, if we felt so strong a need for something which was never there." Of course, we must not push this too far because not everyone feels the urge to worship or that it is necessary to postulate the existence of a Being beyond them. Nevertheless, the idea expressed so beautifully by the Psalmist that "Thou hast set eternity in man's heart" captures something of our restless drive for a divinity which eludes us. The presence of religion since the beginning of time – indeed, some would argue that it is the thing that makes mankind distinctively human – is a factor that cannot easily be brushed aside. And that was Toynbee's point, that the universal striving for "something" beyond us cannot simply be explained by appealing to wish fulfilment.

Further, when we use the word "need" we inevitably give it a narrow meaning of "hunger for God". We find it difficult ever to imagine ourselves saying as some Christians do, "I reached rock bottom, my life was falling apart and Jesus rescued me. I felt suicidal and he was there to help". And, perhaps, we find ourselves thinking, "That's fine for you but what a neurotic mess you were in the first place! That's not for me!" Men, especially, are prone to despise anything which they think is "weak". Now it is true that God meets that kind of need. Many have found God at points of crisis in their lives and God be thanked for stepping in at the nick of time. But not all Christians find their way to faith through that kind of need. I did not and I suspect that the majority do not. We need to give breadth to the idea of "needing God". The kind of breadth I have in mind is caught so well in Augustine's famous saying: "Our hearts are restless until they rest in thee". That is to say, that at the heart of every human self some form of encounter with God is required which is akin to "coming home", the "finding oneself", to becoming fully what we are. And the ways into this centre are so varied and diverse that we can only pick out some of the more popular pathways.

There is the God who makes intellectual sense for us and who becomes the centre of our way of looking at life. For many the Christian way is not the meeting of an emotional need but a wonderful way of seeing the world through companionship with the Maker. So the poet and writer George MacDonald spoke so revealingly about water. "Is oxygen and hydrogen the divine idea of water? God put the two together only that man might separate and find them out? He allows his child to pull his toys to pieces; but were they made that he might pull us to pieces? . . . Find for us what is in the constitution of the two gases, makes them fit and capable to be thus honoured in forming the lovely thing, and you will give us a revelation about more than water, namely about the God who makes oxygen and hydrogen. There is no water in oxygen, no water in hydrogen; it comes bubbling fresh from the imagination of the living God, rushing from the great white throne of the glacier . . . Let him who would know the truth of the Maker, become sorely athirst and drink of the brook by the way – then lift up his heart – not at that moment to the Maker of oxygen and hydrogen, but to the Inventor and Mediator of thirst and water, that man might foresee a little his soul might find in God." Such beautiful words express the poetry of science which is lost once we strip the divine from life.

Then there are those whose need of God has come through the transformation of life. Finding God has led to a total re-ordering of mind, emotions and body in which true "wholeness" has come. They felt quite integrated as people before but now, *all* is well. Somehow the missing link has been found uniting all the diverse parts of their personality and experience. I can think of a senior scientist in one of our leading universities whose discovery of the Christian faith revolutionised his emotional life, thus freeing a rigid and somewhat cold personality resulting not only in the deepening of his personal relationships but also leading to a love of music and art.

Finally, there are those for whom faith has come through its effect on other people – friends, family or acquaintances. So impressed have they been that they themselves have travelled towards God. For them "need" describes what they were missing before. "I had no idea", they might say, "that Christianity could give me such joy or such peace. What I glimpsed through my friend's testimony, I have discovered for myself and what a difference it makes!" What I am saying then is that in such ways our need of God comes not simply through psychological need but through an awareness that without God we have not reached our true stature and destiny. Like most discoveries we only discover what the treasure really is when we find it. That is why those outside the circle always find it so hard to understand what it is that insiders talk about because as yet they cannot share those concerns. Once in, we find the reality which has eluded us and for which we have been searching for years.

The third thing that needs to be said about need is that we must refute the idea that those who need God are somehow inadequate people. No doubt some of us are – whether we are Christian or not. None of us can claim to have advanced to full maturity, or complete humanity, and we would no doubt approve of Charles Spurgeon's wry comment about a man in his congregation: "We all thought our brother was perfect until he told us so!" However, there are a surprising number of people who are not only convinced Christians but are also professional people in society, serving as doctors, teachers, solicitors, scientists, lecturers, Members of Parliament and so on. Not only is this so, but we expect, and often find, that the reality of faith is reflected in changed lives. Any experienced minister will look for signs of God's blessing in a person's life and will find it if faith is genuine. We expect them to be different. We expect people to grow as persons, to become more mature, more self-reliant and able to cope with life's problems. The tree is undoubtedly known by its fruits but the tree has to be there to begin with.

And this last point gets to the heart of what Christian faith is all about. It is not a kind of "coat of mail" which protects inadequate and scared people who have no resources of their own. It is a way of life which is given by God and which makes us the kind of people that God wants us to be. An illustration of the illusions some people have about the Christian life is reflected in a letter written by a man to the theologian Dr J. S. Whale some years ago: "I am 65 years of age, retired after an active life and very happy. My wife is six months younger than me. We have been married forty years very happily. We have never attended church. We have never said a prayer. We neither believe in life after death. We believe in making this world better. Without being egotistical I believe that we have succeeded. We are highly respected by our neighbours, we are not hampered by any creeds but stare life squarely in the face. You might in your talks tell me what religion has to offer us."

I have no idea how Dr Whale replied but essentially here is a self-satisfied man who has already made up his mind that he does not need God. No one would deny his good life but he does not consider it possible that he could be better, that conceivably he might learn something from a faith tested by millions down the centuries, that he could be wrong! I would guess that for such a man the challenge of Christianity will not come to begin with in addition but in subtraction; his pride and self-sufficiency must yield before the claims of Almighty God. He must see himself not as superior to Christians he knows, or religious systems he despises, but alongside Jesus Christ. Once there he will begin to see himself in a different light and begin to discover that what he lacks is not a collection of moral qualities but a relationship to a person.

I am persuaded that what modern people need above all else is an holistic approach to life. Have you noticed the tendency for us to add things on? "It'll be nice to have a bit of religion", we think, and so we start going to church occasionally or we read something uplifting. The mental attitude appears to be politics plus religion, or music plus religion, or science plus religion and by adding things we still subconsciously separate these disciplines into different worlds. But without God there is no wonder, no science, no music, no beauty, no space and no art. It is not a question of adding faith on to what is there but rather allowing faith to transform what is already there, letting it transfuse and irradiate what are God's gifts to us.

Once we begin to see our "need" in terms of wholeness we begin to approach the issue of Christianity in a wholly new way and see it in terms of completion rather than that of inadequacy. But here perhaps Christianity poses its greatest challenge to us because it demands that we get off the fence and do something about it. Indeed, part of the "Great God Robbery" is that we have considered him a thing to argue about rather than Someone to follow and obey. The reason for this assumption is that Western culture has been unduly influenced by the Greek tradition of knowledge rather than the Hebraic way of obedience. The Greek tradition emphasises the process of argument by way of deduction and induction, the sifting of the data and the careful examination of criteria which helps us to arrive at whether God exists or not. Such a process of enquiry at heart is costless; God is yet another object out there who becomes for a short while a subject of examination. Even Christian theology is often guilty of this way of working in its assumption that by conceptual thought God can be known. Now the Greek tradition has a very honourable place in our culture and we are glad of it; much of our science and knowledge would be impossible without this approach. But it is a most inadequate way of knowing God because God is not an object within human knowledge; he is essentially the whole of knowledge. That is to say, he does not exist OUT THERE waiting to be discovered – although that may seem to be the way we find him – but WE EXIST IN HIM and discover that all along we have touched and handled him. So St Paul, preaching to the Greeks in Athens, appeals to one of their own thinkers and recites, "For in him we move and have our being", as a refutation of the folly of proving the existence of the Supreme Being "out there". For St Paul the truth lay rather in God's call and appeal to us to find and know him. The Latin tag "Deus cognitus, Deus nullus" (Known God, no God) conveys a real truth. Once we think we have God buttoned up we are in danger of losing him completely because our tidy systems of thought cannot confine him to the measure of human definitions.

Such an admission may alarm some Christians. "Surely", they will exclaim, "we can find and know God? Isn't that what Christ came to do?" Of course, and I identify with that position gladly and fully, but even in Christ we do not in this life know all there is to know, and the moment any theological system claims to be definitive we stand in danger of losing what we possess.

Then is there a better way? There is I submit and it is to be found in what we might call the "Hebraic tradition" of finding God. Within that tradition, which is the tradition of the Old Testament, the emphasis falls not on intellectual enquiry about God but upon following him. That is to say, whilst the scriptures are not against intellectual study it goes further in demanding a response to God and promising an encounter with the living God. It is fascinating to observe these two completely different traditions of "knowing God". The Greek way is rather static, it assumes that with our reason we may pierce the mists that separate us from God and he will stand revealed. The Hebraic way is more dynamic with God taking the initiative. He does not stand there waiting to be revealed by the mind but he comes to people with moral demands and awaits our response. So the unknown writer of the *Cloud of Unknowing* exclaimed: "By love he may be caught but by thinking never". Such a statement is not an obscurantist brushing aside of thought. It is not true to the general Christian tradition to imply that rigorous intellectual thought is suspect. Indeed, there are many theologians, scholars and teachers for whom the intellectual approach is an important way of knowing God and I include myself in that number. But we would insist that on its own it is a dead end. God's way, the Christian way, requires our response of faith. He is caught by love.

If then we are more or less convinced that the world is rational, that there is sufficient evidence for us to admit it as the work of a Creator, then we are led to ask: "How do I respond? How may I know this God for myself?" To stop here is woefully inadequate. As the theologian John Baillie once laughingly observed: "It is as distressing to the lover to be told that he could not be sure of the existence of his beloved as it is to the devout worshipper to be invited to be content with a merely probable God". Indeed, authentic Christianity does not deal in a merely probable God but in one who is experienced in Jesus Christ.

At this point we are back to our opening question: Do we know enough to place our confidence in the Christian faith? If we accept the probability of God we can go on to test the claims of the One who is for many people in this world the image of the Living God. For to say God is to say Jesus – not that the person of Christ is identical with God – but that God himself is known through Christ. He is the "human face of God" as John Robinson so fittingly put it. So how do we reply to the person who says: "I really want to find God. How do I set out on the road to him?" We must respond, "First get to know the man Jesus. Study the New Testament. Let go of your prejudices. Let him come to you through your reading. Hear his challenge as you open your life to his claims. If you claim to be a decent citizen with no obvious failings or needs, simply stand alongside the person of Jesus Christ and see how you compare. Then, having done that, look at the mystery of his death. Do you not see in it your own death anticipated? Do you not see as you read the New Testament the conviction of the writers that in some mysterious way God in Christ brought you home? Do you not feel the tug of his presence as you study and meditate? Do you not feel disturbed and troubled by this mysterious man on the cross?"

But true Christianity calls us to one further action and that is to follow. Just as there can be·no actual swimming until you take the plunge, there can be no actual believing in God until we are prepared to follow Christ and a twofold commitment is involved in this. First of all we must make our own personal commitment to follow him and that is not easy. We live in a world which, as I observed at the beginning, ignores spiritual values and we feel the drag of this inheritance. To be a Christian in our society is certainly not an easy option. To live His values, to take up our cross in the world, will bring us into conflict with those whose lifestyle and beliefs may be totally alien to Christian standards. Are we prepared to live that kind of life?

The second commitment calls us to identify with the Christian Church. We cannot belong to Christ on our own; it is impossible to be a Robinson Crusoe Christian. We need the human family in order to live and grow and similarly we need the Christian family to grow up as Christians. It is fashionable to despise institutional Christianity. "Jesus – yes; the church – no", was a popular concept among young people a few years back. But to say "Jesus" is to say "Yes" also to his friends and that means those who confess his name. There is of course a lot wrong with the churches and we must not disguise our weakness and poverty. Nevertheless over the years I have discovered the other side of the picture also. Sure, there is a lot wrong with the churches because at heart they reflect ordinary fallible people like you and me. But I for one am proud of the contribution that the Christian Church has made and is making to the store of human knowledge and the welfare of the human family. The fact is that following Jesus does make an enormous difference to the way people live and to the sacrifices they make. I am proud to be a practising Christian because I see first hand the good work that many do in the church in the name of Christ. I see the hundred and more activities which Christians do for him in the world and I am thankful that because of Him millions of Christians are attempting to make this world a better place.

This Jesus, we say, is worth following. He is the human face of God. Follow and find him and you will find God. Don't be conned by the "Great God Robbery".

APPENDIX

As I explained in the introduction I have departed from the tradition of footnotes. The following books have either been quoted in the chapters or are of particular interest if a reader wishes to pursue his enquiries.

CHAPTER 1 *The Great "God" Robbery*

P. Berger *Facing up to Modernity* (Penguin Books, 1977)

P. Berger *A Rumour of Angels* (Pelican, 1969)

T. Roszak *The Making of a Counter Culture* (Faber and Faber, 1970)

B. Ward *The Home of Man* (The Scientific Book Club, 1970)

B. Ward *Faith and Freedom* (Hamish Hamilton, 1954)

H.R. Rookmaaker *Modern Art and the Death of a Culture* (IVP 1970)

J. Bowker *The Sense of God* (Clarendon Press, 1973)

S. Paul Schilling *God in an Age of Unbelief* (Abingdon Press, 1969)

CHAPTER 2 *The Case against God*

H. Montefiore *The Probability of God* (SCM, 1985)

S. Sutherland *Faith and Ambiguity* (SCM, 1984)

P. Vardy *God of Our Fathers?* (DLT, 1987)

J. Baillie *The Sense of the Presence of God* (OUP, 1962)

E.S. Brightman *The Problem of God* (Abingdon Press, 1930)

J. Hick *Existence of God* (Collier Macmillan, 1964)

CHAPTER 3 *Is the Universe on Our Side?*

R. McCormmach *Night Thoughts of a Classical Physicist* (King Penguin, 1982)

P. Lee *Why Believe in God?* (Becket Publications, Oxford, 1983)

The doggerel "There was a hairy baboon" is quoted by Prof. D. Bartholomew in *God of Chance* (SCM, 1984)

P. Davies *God and the New Physics* (Pelican, 1983)

S. W. Hawking *A Brief History of Time* (Bantam Press, 1988)

J. D. Barrow *The World Within the World* (Clarendon Press, 1988) **Strongly commended**

S. Weinberg *The First Three Minutes* (London, 1977)

CHAPTER 4 *A Personal Creator?*

R. Gregory *The Oxford Companion to the Mind* (OUP, 1987)

R. Swinburne *The Existence of God* (Clarendon Press, 1979)

F. Hoyle *The Intelligent Universe* (Michael Joseph, 1983)

W. Paley *The Works of W. Paley*, vol. iv: *Natural Theology* (Oxford, 1938)

R. Swinburne "The Argument for Design", *Philosophy* 43, 1968

P.T. Geach *God and the Soul* (London, 1969)

CHAPTER 5 *Has Life any Meaning?*

B. Lonergan *Method in Theology* (DLT, 1972)

H.P. Owen *The Moral Argument for Christian Theism* (Allen and Unwin, 1965)

O. O'Donovan *Resurrection and Moral Order* (IVP, 1986)

CHAPTER 6 *Good, Evil and God*

B. Lonergan *Philosophy of God and Theology* (DLT, 1973)

J. Neusner *Understanding Jewish Theology* (Ktav Publishing House, New York, 1973)

K. Ward *Rational Theology and the Creativity of God* (Blackwell, 1982)

P. T. Geach *Providence and Evil* (Cambridge University Press, 1977)

J. Hick *Evil and the God of Love* (Macmillan Press, 1977)

CHAPTER 7 *What has Experience to say about God?*

F.C. Happold *Religious Faith and Twentieth Century Man* (Pelican, 1966)

A. O'Hear *Experience, Explanation and Faith* (Routledge, 1984)

CHAPTER 8 *The Case against Unbelief*

D. Bartholomew *God of Chance* (SCM, 1984)

Del Ratzsch *Philosophy of Science* (IVP, 1986)

D. Nicholl "What Sort of Universe?" (*The Tablet*, 2nd April 1988 and the two following editions)

CHAPTER 9 *What Kind of God?*

N. Pittenger *Picturing God* (SCM, 1982)

N. Pittenger *Process Thought and Christian Faith* (J. Nisbet and Co., 1968)

B. Davies *Thinking About God* (Geoffrey Chapman, 1985)

G. O'Collins *Interpreting Jesus* (Geoffrey Chapman, 1983)

D. Day *This Jesus* (IVP, 1983)

CHAPTER 10 *What Kind of Response?*

C. Lamb *Jesus Through Other Eyes* (Latimer Studies 14, Oxford, 1982)

E. Schillebeeckx *Jesus in Our Western Culture* (SCM, 1986)

N. Anderson *The Mystery of the Incarnation* (Hodder and Stoughton, 1978)

T. Torrance *Time, Space and Incarnation* (OUP, 1969)

Also available in Fount Paperbacks

BOOKS BY C. S. LEWIS

The Abolition of Man

'It is the most perfectly reasoned defence of Natural Law (Morality) I have ever seen, or believe to exist.'

Walter Hooper

Mere Christianity

'He has a quite unique power for making theology an attractive, exciting and fascinating quest.'

Times Literary Supplement

God in the Dock

'This little book . . . consists of some brilliant pieces . . . This is just the kind of book to place into the hands of an intellectual doubter . . . It has been an unalloyed pleasure to read.'

Marcus Beverley, Christian Herald

The Great Divorce

'Mr Lewis has a rare talent for expressing spiritual truth in fresh and striking imagery and with uncanny acumen . . . it contains many flashes of deep insight and exposures of popular fallacies.'

Church Times

Also available in Fount Paperbacks

The Mind of St Paul
WILLIAM BARCLAY

'There is a deceptive simplicity about this fine exposition of Pauline thought at once popular and deeply theological. The Hebrew and Greek backgrounds are described and all the main themes are lightly but fully treated.'   *The Yorkshire Post*

The Plain Man Looks at the Beatitudes
WILLIAM BARCLAY

'. . . the author's easy style should render it . . . valuable and acceptable to the ordinary reader.'   *Church Times*

The Plain Man Looks at the Lord's Prayer
WILLIAM BARCLAY

Professor Barclay shows how this prayer that Jesus gave to his disciples is at once a summary of Christian teaching and a pattern for all prayers.

The Plain Man's Guide to Ethics
WILLIAM BARCLAY

The author demonstrates beyond all possible doubt that the Ten Commandments are the most relevant document in the world today and are totally related to mankind's capacity to live and make sense of it all within a Christian context.

Ethics in a Permissive Society
WILLIAM BARCLAY

How do we as Christians deal with such problems as drug taking, the 'pill', alcohol, morality of all kinds, in a society whose members are often ignorant of the Church's teaching? Professor Barclay approaches a difficult and vexed question with his usual humanity and clarity, asking what Christ himself would say or do in our world today.

Fount Paperbacks

Fount is one of the leading paperback publishers of religious books and below are some of its recent titles.

- ☐ THROUGH SEASONS OF THE HEART
  John Powell £4.95
- ☐ WORDS OF LIFE FROM JOHN THE BELOVED
  Frances Hogan £2.95
- ☐ MEISTER ECKHART Ursula Fleming £2.95
- ☐ CHASING THE WILD GOOSE Ron Ferguson £2.95
- ☐ A GOOD HARVEST Rita Snowden £2.50
- ☐ UNFINISHED ENCOUNTER Bob Whyte £5.95
- ☐ FIRST STEPS IN PRAYER Jean-Marie Lustiger £2.95
- ☐ IF THIS IS TREASON Allan Boesak £2.95
- ☐ RECLAIMING THE CHURCH Robin Greenwood £2.95
- ☐ GOD WITHIN US John Wijngaards £2.95
- ☐ GOD'S WORLD Trevor Huddleston £2.95
- ☐ A CALL TO WITNESS Oliver McTernan £2.95
- ☐ GOODNIGHT LORD Georgette Butcher £2.95
- ☐ FOR GOD'S SAKE Donald Reeves £3.50
- ☐ GROWING OLDER Una Kroll £2.95
- ☐ THROUGH THE YEAR WITH FRANCIS OF ASSISI
  Murray Bodo £2.95

All Fount Paperbacks are available at your bookshop or newsagent, or they can be ordered by post from Fount Paperbacks, Cash Sales Department, G.P.O. Box 29, Douglas, Isle of Man. Please send purchase price plus 22p per book, maximum postage £3. Customers outside the UK send purchase price, plus 22p per book. Cheque, postal order or money order. No currency.

NAME (Block letters) _____

ADDRESS_____

_____

_____